THE LESSON OF THE MASTER

Norman Thomas di Giovanni

The Lesson of the Master

A Memoir and Essays on Borges
and His Work

NEW EDITION,
REVISED AND ENLARGED

FRIDAY
BOOKS

The Friday Project
An imprint of HarperCollins Publishers
77–85 Fulham Palace Road
Hammersmith, London W6 8JB
www.thefridayproject.co.uk
www.harpercollins.co.uk

First published in 2003 by Continuum
This edition published in 2011 by The Friday Project

A catalogue record for this book is available
from the British Library

ISBN 978-0-00-735859-5

Designed and typeset by Marcial Souto,
Barcelona and Buenos Aires

To Pamela Griffiths

Contents

Foreword   11

Foreword to the First Edition   17

I

In Memory of Borges   23

II

Borges and His Interpreters   59

Borges at Play: The Self and the Selves   77

Evaristo Carriego: Borges as Biographer   109

Borges and His Sources: *A Universal History
   of Infamy*   133

Borges and His Autobiography   165

On Translating Borges   185

A Translator's Guide   209

Backward Glances   217

Afterword   229

Appendix: A Footnote to Infamy   233

Contents

Foreword

Apologia to the First Edition

In Memory of Borges

II

Borges and His Interpreters

Borges at Play: The Self and the Selves

Evaristo Carriego: Borges as Biographer   168

Borges and His Sources, Critics and Theory
of Influence

Borges and His Autobiography

On Translating Borges

A Translator's Guide

Index of Names

Afterword

Appendix: A Foreword to Inferno

Foreword

The roots of this book go back exactly a decade, to when Buenos Aires was plunged into the circus celebrations of the Borges centenary. The affair, designated *el año borgeano* – the Year of Borges – was arranged to span twelve months.

The festivities began on the twenty-fourth of August 1998, the date of the master's ninety-ninth birthday, with an evening of 'anecdotes and testimony' at Buenos Aires' San Martín Cultural Centre. Here, Borges was remembered by friends and – most incongruously – by politicians, a breed he held in utter contempt.

Two days later, as reported in the pages of *La Nación*, a book to herald the Year of Years was launched at the city's Museum of Decorative Arts. The volume, an illustrated edition of *El Aleph*, Borges's best collection of stories, was an extravaganza of bookmaking. Twelve years in production, the tome was limited to twenty-five copies and was on sale for $25,000. The artwork employed, among other techniques, watercolour, etching, lithography, pencil, oil, and acrylic. The enterprise was masterminded by two Argentine magnates – one the founder of a ski resort and the other an ex-industrialist in metals. *La Nación* went on to describe the book as

unique of its kind because each copy has been painted in an exclusive way, leaf by leaf. No one of the 4,000 pages that make up the edition is like any other.

It was a case of life imitating art. A few years earlier, Borges had devised a Book of Sand, consisting of an infinite number of pages of which none was the first and none the last. The volume bore countless small illustrations two thousand pages apart, but no one of them could be found twice. Borges dubbed his creation monstrous, 'a nightmarish object, an obscene thing'.

My own book, translated as *La lección del maestro*, appeared in Buenos Aires in the wake of this year-long apotheosis. The city, in 2003, was still basking in the heady afterglow of Borges's deification. Several reviewers therefore angrily rounded on me; to them, my essays laid a heretical claim to my having sat at the right hand of God. That was of course both absurd and impossible. The Borges I had written about was the Borges of several decades earlier, who was then only a god-in-waiting.

I did not fare much better with certain English reviewers, who seemed unable to believe that I could have played the part I described in Borges's life. The memoir about this, 'In Memory of Borges', was written from jottings in notebooks of the period. In their breezy shorthand I wanted to reflect the rush of our lives, of our compressed and packed days. I also wanted to provide examples of the sort of playful irony and humour that Borges and I shared and that were his hallmarks. This somehow rankled. When I wrote, meaning just the opposite, that a certain article in a Buenos Aires weekly was about *me* and not about Borges, the essay was branded 'quite transparently a work of aggrieved limelight seeking.' Unfortunately the reviewer had missed the joke. I'd never had to seek the limelight with Borges because from the outset of my career with him I had been thrust into it.

'Some Borges aficionados are irritated (to put it mildly)', wrote another critic, 'that di Giovanni's association with Borges developed from the role of passive translator to active collaborator.' Borges himself had no such qualms. He once told an audience, 'When we attempt a translation, or re-creation, of my poems or prose in English, we don't think of ourselves as being two men. We think we are really one mind at work.' For 'irritated', perhaps 'envious' would have been the better word choice – again the right-hand-of-God syndrome.

Someone else found the book 'burdened with grudges' and complained that I had 'scores to settle with executors, editors, translators and academics, who are accused of being mean-minded, middling, incompetent and obfuscating respectively.' On one of these counts I do bear a grudge, and why should I not air it? Decades of my work, a significant portion of it also Borges's, have been consigned to the dustbin. His executor refused to honour Borges's word; I was informed by the American publisher of his fiction that 'the estate would not allow us to republish Borges under the old ... terms.' On the spot, my formal contractual agreements of twenty or more years were unilaterally declared null and void.

Nor have I been the only person incensed about this turn of events. Many readers of Borges, some of whom vent their views on the Internet, also feel cheated. Susan Sontag even took the trouble to write to me that

As a fervent Borgesian, I purchased the Viking Penguin three volumes the moment they came out. And it was obvious to me, just reading here and there among old favorites ... that the whole enterprise was incoherent and *indigne*. Contemptible. A travesty.

A word about 'A Translator's Guide'. An Argentine reviewer berated me for *not* naming the errant translators quoted in the text. But my purpose was not to blacken the reputation of any individual, only to draw attention to certain common failings and pitfalls that plague most prose translation. As stated in the piece, I was attempting to throw a lifeline to monolingual publishers' editors and, possibly, to the apprentice translator.

Readers of 'Borges and His Autobiography' must be let in on something that I deliberately omitted the first time round. The Barcelona firm that tried to publish the autobiography without my permission was forced to lock horns with me in a protracted lawsuit. They did not dispute that I owned fifty per cent of the said work but claimed that Borges had made me a gift of it. Of necessity they held that I was not its co-author. (At stake in this distinction – for them – was the matter of my damages.) María Kodama, executor of the Borges Estate, waded in with an affidavit stating that *it did not seem to her* that I had co-written the essay. Why should it have seemed so to her? When the piece was composed, in 1970, she did not occupy centre-stage in Borges's life and had no idea what he and I were up to in our daily work sessions.

The publisher's claims were all the more bizarre when set alongside the introduction to the book by its translator, the Latin-American professor Aníbal González. He pointed out that the autobiography 'is the product of a collaboration with another writer, the translator di Giovanni. It is, then, not just a text written in another language but also in part, literally, by someone else.'

To close this sordid episode on a sunny note, let me report that the Spanish Supreme Court – thanks to the efforts of my lawyer Alejandro Angulo – eventually found in my favour.

I am often asked to write brief comments or reminiscences about my Borges years. Three such pieces, under the collective title 'Backward Glances', have been added here to close this new edition. Their histories are as follows.

'A Reader's Life', commissioned by Erica Wagner as a review of James Woodall's *The Man in the Mirror of the Book*, first appeared under the title 'Trapped inside the house of fame' in *The Times*, 11 July 1996.

'Borges Remembered', commissioned by Sophy Roberts, first appeared under the title 'Borges and Me' in *Departures*, October 2006.

'The Other Borges', commissioned by Khademul Islam, first appeared in the *Daily Star*, Dhaka, 20 June 2009.

The three were also printed together in the *Raconteur*, Winter 2010, under the title 'Backward Glances: Remembering Borges'.

Warm thanks are due to Marcial Souto, to Susan Ashe, and to my son Tom di Giovanni for sage counsel, editorial and otherwise. Finally, for being the Maecenas of this book's second edition, I want to express my gratitude to Scott Pack, of The Friday Project, an obvious maverick who does not shrink from the company of fellow mavericks.

Norman Thomas di Giovanni
Keyhaven, Lymington
Hampshire
November 2009

Foreword to the First Edition

The twenty-fourth of August 1999, marked the centenary of the birth of Jorge Luis Borges, the Argentine's best known and one of its greatest literary figures.

Some thirty years ago, while he was delivering a series of public addresses at Harvard University, our paths crossed, we began working together on translations of his work into English, and we became friends. Looking back now, I find that the impact of Borges on the course of my life seems to have been only inches short of a miracle. Within a few brief months of our meeting, publishers began to compete for his stories and poems and essays in the new versions of them that we were making. On the eve of his return to Buenos Aires, in April 1968, he invited me to join him in his country, and seven months later I was there, plunged into the thick of his life and into the life of Argentina.

All that is a story yet to be told. Back then, while these events were unfolding, everything was hectic and crowded, and I was offered no leisure for reflection. Yet never once was I unaware of how rich and marvellous was life alongside Borges. So rich and indelible were those days of our close association, in fact, that even now, over a decade after his death, he still inhabits most of my working hours and occasionally, at night, even my dreams.

The little memoir and the essays collected here are in the nature of a homage and a contribution to the celebration of Borges's life and work. The book is no attempt to deliver the final word on him or on any aspect of what he wrote. Offering simple guidance and a commonsensical approach to reading him, the pieces are more tentative and modest. In most ways, these pages are the close-up view, the record, of someone who worked on a daily basis with Borges at a distinctive and critical period of his life, when he overcame various adversities and experienced a rich late flowering.

The Lesson of the Master has had a singular genesis. At the outset of our association, when Borges and I were working on an English edition of his selected poems, he described me in a letter to his Buenos Aires publisher, the late Carlos Frías, as the volume's 'onlie begetter'. It was a term that both men, teachers of English literature, savoured.

Originally, I wanted to publish the memoir that opens the present volume as a tailpiece to Borges's 'Autobiographical Essay', a 20,000-word text that he and I composed together in English, in 1970. The Borges Estate, however, did not look kindly on the idea. No explanation, no reasons, were given for their decision, but somehow my work of 1988 was not deemed worthy of appearing alongside my work with Borges of 1970. An Argentine editor came along, however, and said that he would undertake to publish the two essays separately.

Working with Borges, one had come to appreciate the fact that less was more, but my thirty-odd-page essay, I thought to myself, was about to become the slimmest book on record. Marcial Souto, my mentor in these matters and himself a minimalist in literary creation, was also apprehensive. (It was he who had brought the original project to the Argentine editor's attention.) Souto suggested that I couple with the memoir some other related piece or pieces of mine. I sent him a further essay, twenty pages long, and he approved. For a month or two after, I was haunted by the melancholy notion that – when all I wanted was to bring out a volume worthy of the master – I was about to become holder of the even less distinguished record of producing the *second* slimmest book in publishing history. This would not do. Ransacking my papers, I began to turn up the material that eventually made its way into the present pages. It is in this roundabout way, then, that the Borges Estate is the 'onlie begetter' of these essays. To the Estate and to Mr Souto, my thanks.

Norman Thomas di Giovanni
October 1999

I

In Memory of Borges

There is an article, really a piece of photojournalism, in one of those Argentine weekly magazines, in which I can be seen walking down a Buenos Aires street with Borges leaning on my arm. Was the magazine *Siete Días* or *Gente*? That I no longer remember, but all the other details I am fairly clear about. It was 1969; we were walking east along Belgrano Avenue, crossing Santiago del Estero or more likely Salta, a block or two from the small flat where Borges was still living with his first wife. I am wearing my brown herringbone tweed suit and a tie, concessions to the demands of sober, formal Buenos Aires. We are crossing or about to cross Salta, Borges clutching my right arm in his somewhat frantic blind man's vice, and the large photograph in the magazine is a picture of me with him on my arm and definitely not the other way round – it is not a photograph of Borges being led along by some anonymous younger man, a foreigner, an American.

That year, on the dot of four every afternoon, five days a week, I picked Borges up from the Belgrano flat and, his arm firmly gripping mine, we walked the ten slow blocks east to the National Library, in Mexico Street, where our early evening's work awaited us. By this time, he had been Director of the Argentine National Library for fourteen years. The post, of course, was a sinecure. Borges was not a librarian, much less an administrator, and a loyal assistant director, José Edmundo Clemente, did the real work. Once or twice a month perhaps, like a ritual, a secretary came into the big office where Borges and I sat across from each other at a solid long mahogany table, and she would stand over a thick sheaf of papers, turning a corner of each page for him to initial. Whatever the bulk of paperwork, it never proved much of an interruption. Most of the time he initialled away while carrying on his discussion with me; but if things were going particularly well and he was in one of his playful moods, which were frequent, he might indulge in a bit of good-natured ribbing, poking fun at her to me in English or at me to her in Spanish.

'You see, di Giovanni, how mercilessly she makes me work.' Often the woman would be halfway out of the room before Borges would remember himself and, for form's sake, think to ask exactly what it was he had just signed.

'Only the usual accounts, Señor Borges,' she would say assuringly, the epitome of correctness and respect.

'Ah, yes,' he would rejoin, as if suddenly reminded of some immutable truth.

It was a game. The secretaries, one or two in the morning, a different one or two in the afternoon, hated troubling Borges about anything, especially when he was working, and to this day I am sure that even after it had been explained to him Borges never had the foggiest notion what he was signing.

'Borges,' I'd quip when the mood came over me, 'I can see from here that that sheaf you're putting your John Hancock to grants the whole library staff an extra two-week holiday with pay.'

And he would do a comic double-take, feigning astonishment, stop scribbling, look up trying to locate the secretary's face, and repeat to her my remark in Spanish.

'*No, jamás nunca, Señor Borges; le juro.*' And with her oaths to the contrary and not-on-your-lifes, he let himself be readily convinced every time.

This is not to suggest that Borges did not take the job in earnest. He did. But at the same time he knew he was a figurehead – a mere figurehead, he would have phrased it – and, never pompous about anything, he allowed himself to be ironic about the post. Deep down, he was proud of the library, of the position, and grateful for it too. Almost in the manner of a credulous child, he would recite for visitors that the library contained 800,000 volumes. Or later, 900,000. It was one of the few facts Borges ever had at his fingertips. To him facts were the antithesis of the essence of truth, and he found them meaningless.

This was the only fact I can remember his spouting that required – unlike the year of his birth, say – frequent updating. The job was the perfect symbol for him, and he was the perfect symbol for the job. Indeed, what library in the world would not have rejoiced at having a Borges as its titular head? He performed the office like a master – as if he had been born to it, or, better, because he had been born to it.

Those evenings of ours were devoted to the translation of stories, poems, and essays of his into English. 'My afternoons now are usually given over to a long-range and cherished project,' Borges was to write a year later, when he was seventy-one. 'For nearly the past three years, I have been lucky to have my own translator at my side, and together we are bringing out some ten or twelve volumes of my work in English, a language I am unworthy to handle, a language I often wish had been my birthright.'

As the young man from *Siete Días* or *Gente* knew, all this made a good story: the American from Boston who had suddenly popped up and was shepherding the legendary Borges along the streets of Buenos Aires and working with him at the National Library. In fact, the story had a bit of everything – the exotic and the homely. Here was the lofty National Treasure, for whom New York publishers were competing, whom they had sent one of their own to the ends of the earth to watch over. It proved Borges really was a world figure and not just an oddball local, an

Anglophile with a passion for books; it meant that Buenos Aires and Argentina counted in the world for something more than excellent steaks and crack football players. It was a fine tonic for the constant doubt about his identity that assails the *porteño* at the best of times. These were not the best of times. 'Nationalism is creeping in all the time,' Borges sneered. It was the military dictatorship of General Onganía; soon grim-faced Federal police, more of them every week, would be appearing on street corners wearing jackboots and wielding stubby submachine guns; soon the faithful flock would be bleating for the return of Perón. With the horizon fast shading from leaden to black, enter the young American in the tweed suit who had something in common with half the population of Buenos Aires – a comforting Italian surname. Which was why the story was about me, why the pictures were of me with the National Treasure on *my* arm and not of Borges with me on his.

I often joked with him about this. As we moved through Florida Street, a pedestrian precinct on the way to his mother's, people would open a way, turn round, gape, point. 'It never ceases to amaze me the way strangers seem to recognize me,' I would tell him, deadpan. "Look," they say, "there's di Giovanni – there, with the old man on his arm."' It made Borges laugh every time. The passers-by never failed to greet him; some even held their children up for him to touch. He always asked people their names, where they were from. Ah, yes. He had a friend there. A lawyer and a fine poet named Fernández Ordóñez. Borges was a living monument, and the Argentines revered him.

At the library we shuffled through the revolving door and up the grand marble staircase, entering first the outer office with the scruffy, bare, wooden floor, where the secretaries huddled at a tiny table in the corner by the window. Except by that window, the room was lightless, bleak, and spartan. A small wire wastebasket stood beside the table. There was one telephone – big, clumsy, black, its cord frayed. It didn't matter. The phones, like the secretaries, only worked part-time. The building dated from 1901 and had been, as Borges was fond of telling visitors, the seat of the national lottery. The inner sanctum, Borges's office, had an extraordinarily high ceiling, green wallpaper printed with bamboo-like fronds, polished mahogany panelling, and a parquet floor. We worked at the old-fashioned conference table in the centre of the room. At the far end was the desk that Paul Groussac, a distinguished predecessor, had had built to his own design. It was U-shaped. If you sat behind it, as Borges never did, it surrounded you. It had strange drawers and odd compartments. Borges later described it briefly at the end of his story 'There Are More Things'.

The room's other furnishings were a couple of revolving bookshelves and a tall set of drawers into which Borges slipped the drafts of poems he dictated in the morning to a secretary. Two pairs of doors led off the room straight onto a corridor. These we used only when trying to give the slip to someone who might be waiting in the outer office or when we went to the vast, stark loo that was used only by us. Next door was the room Groussac had died in, a detail Borges took ghoulish delight in recounting. For once upon a time the director had lived on the premises. There were traces of a kitchen that proved it. But Elsa, the new Mrs Borges, whom Borges had married at sixty-eight (she was some ten or twelve years younger), would have none of it. She was right, of course. The library was a gloomy place, and I thought I too would go blind there. There was a dictionary of the Spanish Royal Academy, whose paper and binding Borges and I were fond of smelling, on the main table. The one place in all Buenos Aires where my tweed suit was no match for the winter was in the dank cavern of Borges's office. But there was a large, ornate fireplace at my back, where a fire of eucalyptus logs would glow – not burn but glow. If I backed up to it now and again, the icy chill was momentarily dispelled. Still, one was thankful for small mercies.

What the photographs in the magazine article do not show is the crablike walk I had developed, much to the detriment of my lower back muscles. Buenos Aires pavements are narrow, and to negotiate them with Borges on my right arm I had to learn to master the art of walking with my left hip and left arm leading the way. To make matters worse, my extended left hand always carried a briefcase bulging with papers and books. There I was with the National Treasure on my arm, keeping him safe from the murderous traffic, the ubiquitous excavations, and the broken tiles of the city's pavements, steering him round open pits or dodging beau traps. And all the while the squat buses inched along in step with us, throbbing and belching thick black exhaust over the Treasure; over my herringbone tweed; over his monologue about Victoria Ocampo, whom he dubbed Queen Victoria for her imperial ways, or Ernesto Sabato, dubbed the Dostoyevsky of Santos Lugares for his bouts of melancholia; over an example of the word music of Dunbar, Coleridge, or the Bard himself, whose 'multitudinous seas incarnadine', capped with 'making the green one red', never failed to rouse and thrill Borges – potholes, pitfalls, grime, soot, lethal traffic, and sputtering buses be damned.

Once, fourteen years later and forty miles away across the river in Uruguay, in the town of Colonia, where I was helping make a BBC film about Borges, I stumbled across a half-open gateway that gave a glimpse of a picturesque garden with a big fig tree ripening in the middle of it. I couldn't resist. In I strolled, utterly captivated. Immediately a man dashed out of a house, a stern look on his face, to halt me in my tracks.

'*Lo felicito,*' I said in my most winning Spanish, trying to disarm him. 'I congratulate you; your garden is a jewel.'

He drew up to me, tall, handsome, almost sneering, an obvious *porteño*. Then the belligerence drained from his look.

'*Yo te conozco a vos,*' he said straight out, launching into the familiar. 'I saw you walking down Calle Florida in 1969 or 1970 with Borges on your arm.'

There are jottings in a series of diaries, the old War Resisters League peace calendars I was partial to at the time, in which I chronicled those first teeming weeks in Buenos Aires after I arrived there in the middle of November 1968. Borges was tireless in showing me the same hospitality in his country that he had thanked me for showing him in mine, when we had parted in Cambridge, Massachusetts, seven months before.

He and Elsa met my plane at Ezeiza on the night I got there and whisked me straight to the modest hotel she had found for me in the Avenida de Mayo, a short walk from their flat. The next day, after lunch with them, Borges could barely wait to show me the National Library and a few spots nearby, on the old south side of the city, that he both worshipped and had turned into myth. A house from the previous century; a grilled archway; a long street of low houses; a dusty park. 'After all, these places mean a great deal to me; they're my past.' It was touching the way he apologized for the absence of grandeur or glamour he thought that I, as a Bostonian, had a right to expect. But that was politeness. Beneath the courtesy, you were aware of his intense personal pride.

We began work at the library the next morning, a Saturday, when the library was closed, for that had been the pact. I would not come as a tourist; I would only come if we could continue what we had begun at Harvard during the months we had known each other there. The diary for 1968 records that we busied ourselves on his poem 'Heraclitus'.

That same day he introduced me to a student of his, María Kodama, whom he was to marry seventeen and a half years later, only weeks before his death. And that night, my second full evening in Argentina, he took me to dine at the home of Adolfo Bioy Casares, where I was presented to some of Borges's closest friends. This was an event I had been looking forward to for months; from the warmth of the reception I received from Bioy and his wife, Silvina Ocampo, I realized Borges had talked to them about me. Bioy and Silvina were both writers – he of novels and stories, she of stories and poems (she was also an accomplished artist who had studied with de Chirico) – and together they and Borges had collaborated on a variety of literary projects. Manuel Peyrou, the novelist, was also there, and towards the end of the meal Teddy Paz, one of the younger literati, ambled in. That evening, that dinner, was truly auspicious, but not just for me, because it marked the start of four enduring new friendships. Bioy got his car out and drove us home at one a.m. By then something had happened to make it one of the most important evenings in Borges's life.

During those final weeks of his stay in Cambridge, where he had been delivering the 1967–8 Charles Eliot Norton Lectures and we had been preparing an English edition of his selected poems, we had read together and chosen and made literal drafts of dozen upon dozen of Borges's sonnets, a form he increasingly favoured, since he could easily write them in his head. I knew that. But it did not keep me from wearying of those same fourteen hendecasyllabic lines, the inevitability of those seven pairs of rhymes. The very constriction, in fact, was giving me claustrophobia. I told him so – not that it would alter the shape of our project in any way. I told him simply because I saw no one else come forward, even once, and tell him the truth. Every poem, tale, or essay he had ever written was hailed a masterpiece; each of his utterances, on whatever subject, seemed to have cast a spell over academics the length and breadth of America. To me, he confessed his fears, his inadequacies. He felt he would never write again; so did America. Borges's isolation was cruel, crippling, and complete. He was high up on a pedestal, a monument.

He listened and explained, by rote, that sonnets

were all he could now manage. He was not vehement, nor was I. I simply reminded him by their titles of some fine poems written during his blindness that were not sonnets, and no more was said. But within a month or two of his return to Buenos Aires, Elsa began posting me at regular intervals a series of poems that were new and fresh – and not a sonnet among them. By the time I reached Buenos Aires, I was in possession of seventeen uncollected poems.

'Are these all recent poems, or is this work you found in some bottom drawer?' I asked him on the morning we tackled 'Heraclitus'.

'Why?' he said in a panic. 'Don't you like them?'

'They're marvellous.'

'Ah, that's a relief,' Borges said. 'You see, I was doing what you told me to do back in Cambridge.'

'Yes, and it means you have half a new book here.'

'No, no!' he protested, flying into a rage. 'I won't publish another book. I haven't published a new book in eight years and I won't be judged by this stuff.'

He was beside himself in a way I had never seen before. It was a hot potato, and I let it drop.

But over dinner the next night at Bioy's he blurted out aggressively, 'Di Giovanni has a crazy idea. He wants me to publish a new book of poems.' It was the manner he used, I was to learn, when he found himself on unsure ground but wanted to give the opposite impression.

'But, Georgie,' Bioy immediately chimed in,

chuckling his infectious little chuckle. 'That seems to me a splendid idea.'

Silvina agreed; Peyrou agreed. I had no need to add a word.

One day the next week, there was an unexpected phone call from Borges, with a hint of mystery in his voice, saying he had an errand to run that morning and would I meet him at the library a bit later on. When around midday we eventually got together again, he was jubilant. 'I've been to see Frías,' he said. Carlos Frías was his editor at Emecé. 'I told him, "Frías, I want to publish a new book of poems."' Again the aggressive tone.

'Let me guess his decision,' I said, playing the straight man. 'He accepted.'

Borges was stunned and momentarily deflated. 'Yes. How did you know?'

That did it. His mind was made up. He was writing a new book and he wanted everyone to know he was writing a new book. 'Thirty-four poems, eh? You think that's about right, do you? That's the figure I gave Frías. Now you're sure we have seventeen. Let's go over that list of yours once again.'

We went over the list, which he learned by heart, ticking each title off on his fingers. What this meant, I told him, was that from then on we would work together only in the afternoons. He must devote his mornings to dictating new work. Borges offered no demur.

That was a skirmish. The real battle loomed ahead – the bits of evidence are there in the diary jottings – but I would not be aware of this for another six months. The entry for 4 December 1968 relates that in the evening we went out to Palermo, the neighbourhood of Buenos Aires where Borges had grown up, and we walked around the streets before going around the corner to eat *empanadas* at the home of Elsa's cousin Olga.

'Don't expect anything now,' Borges had prefaced the journey in his characteristic way.

It was a year and a day since we had first met. We stopped at an old *almacén*, where two men played with a pack of greasy cards at a plain wooden table. The place was ill-lit and nearly empty. Borges asked for a couple of *cañas quemadas*, an old-fashioned rum-like liqueur. Afterwards, outside, he confessed, 'I asked for a small one because a big one would have defeated me.' He told me he hadn't been out this way for thirty years. Then, like an eager schoolboy, he showed me a narrow, cobbled alleyway, pointing out that it was untypical for running in a diagonal instead of forming the side of a square. And on the spot he began recounting the 'plot of a story that has the ghost of Juan Muraña as a protagonist.' (An entry in a pocket notebook tells me this.) But of course he at once lamented the fact that, though he might still compose poems, he would never set down this story, since there was no way he could ever manage to write prose again. I gave him a sympathetic ear.

He and Elsa were invited to Israel for a few weeks early in the new year, and he came back full of wry little stories about the Holy Land. The Israelis, one notebook jotting tells me, were 'a bunch of Russians or Germans in disguise, playing at being characters out of the Old Testament – Noahs.' But he was elated. He was working, which in Borges's terms meant justifying his existence. And, what was more, harder than ever before in his life. (This was Bioy's observation; he had close to forty years' experience of Borges's habits.) Mornings were spent working on new poems for his book, dictating them to a secretary. In February, our afternoons were given over to a translation and rewriting of the long series of miniature essays that made up *The Book of Imaginary Beings*. By then I had burned my bridges and decided to stay on in Argentina longer than the five months I had initially planned. We finished the *Imaginary Beings* on 20 May 1969; he was so delighted with the result that any future translation of the book, he insisted, must be based on our English version. He also insisted that we now celebrate the end of the job by writing some new pieces for the book directly in English. We concocted four, working into them all manner of silly things, like the long Dutch name of one of my friends, a family surname, and my Buenos Aires street and flat number. It was all in good fun and the kind of thing Borges took delight in. Three days later, we wrapped the book up with a new foreword;

three days after that, the typescript was winging its way to New York.

'*Norteamérica*,' Borges told the pillarbox, giving it an affectionate pat. 'I always tell the box where the letter goes. Otherwise, how would it know?'

The jotting in the peace calendar for this year tells that on 11 June Borges and I had worked on pages 17–19 of his 1951 short story 'Ibn Hakkan al-Bokhari, Dead in His Labyrinth', and that that evening we took a taxi out to his publishers in the two thousand block of Alsina to turn in the last poem of his new book *Elogio de la sombra – In Praise of Darkness*. An emendation added later in brackets records that 'more material was turned in after this date.' This was his fifth book of poems, he was to write in his foreword to the volume later that month, and to 'the mirrors, mazes, and swords which my re-signed reader already foresees, two new themes have been added: old age and ethics.' As it turned out, there was something else in the book too – a grain of sand that would make a pearl. This was a story, not a prose poem, no more than three or four pages long about a man who hides out in a cellar for nine years.

Borges's lament about not being able to write down short stories that he was for ever working out in his head did not end after our Palermo excursion. Over the next months these stories became a more and more frequent topic of conversation on our walks to and from the library. At some point – but this was much later on – I began keeping track of them; by then the list I drew up numbered eight. That autumn (it was the southern hemisphere) I no longer just lent a silent ear but began a subtle campaign of egging him on, shoring up his confidence, and proving to him that his writing days were far from over. I had two arrows in my quiver. One was the five-page story 'The Intruder' that he had dictated to his ancient mother three years earlier; the other was the recent 'Pedro Salvadores', the man in the cellar.

'Sure you can,' I'd point out. 'After all, the difference in length between "The Intruder" and any of your other stories is a bare page or two.'

This was a slight exaggeration, perhaps, but he never opposed the argument. On the contrary, my persuasiveness made him open up, and he began using me as a sounding board for yet another tale whose plot he now wove aloud to me. And he'd ask my opinion of specific elements – should he add another incident? Were the main characters different enough?

I never tried to supply answers but would raise more questions. 'What are the alternatives?' I kept wanting him to tell me.

He'd ponder, come up with an idea, and we'd kick it around. I knew he was girding himself and working up to something; and I was determined to feed his mood whilst not letting him off the hook.

Then, at his doorstep: 'No, I fear it's too late in the day; I don't think I could manage it.'

'Tommyrot,' I'd say. His Edwardian slang, as I called it, was one of our pet jokes. 'Why not try? It's a good story. It's only a matter of writing "Pedro Salvadores" twice. Eight pages. You can do it.'

And on and on it went for several weeks. One day, in the midst of this, Manuel Peyrou rang from *La Prensa*, where he worked as an editor, to tell Borges that the paper was celebrating its centenary later in the year and was inviting every Argentine writer of note to contribute to a succession of special Sunday supplements. Here was another turning point. Not long after this, Borges took a poem around to them. But the next day, rather than feeling good about it, he was actually glum.

'I don't think a poem's what they had in mind,' he said.

'What do you mean?'

'I think they'd like a story.'

'Of course they'd like a story. We'd all like a story. Why not write them one?'

I never for a moment believed *La Prensa* was unhappy with his poem; certainly Peyrou knew that Borges had more or less given up writing stories since 1953. This was Borges having a pang of conscience. *La Prensa* had offered him the same fee whether they got a poem or a story out of him, and he felt he had cheated them. Whatever the truth of the matter, the mysterious strands were coming together fast now.

It became an open secret at the library that Borges was dictating a full-length short story; he knew I knew, but superstitiously he refused to breathe a word of it to me. He didn't have to, as the team of secretaries gave me daily reports. It went through two or three drafts and took him two or three weeks to write. He finally came clean when he'd finished, but he made no offer to show me the result. I bided my time.

A few days later I lied and told him I was short of money. Reaching for the billfold he kept in his inside breast pocket, he asked how much I needed. No, I laughed, what I had in mind was the new story, which I wanted to translate and sell to the *New Yorker*, where our work had been appearing. This took place on a Monday. All right, he said, but not that day. I would have to wait until Friday.

There was no earthly reason for his not handing me the story then and there, except that as the remote possibility did exist that Friday might never come round he could actually trick himself into believing he would escape having to stand judgement. It was complicated; it was capricious; it was Borges.

But that Friday did come round – according to my diary it was 16 May – and the delivery could be put off no longer. After our afternoon's ration of *Imaginary Beings* and just before we knocked off, he put the typescript in my hands, saying, 'Don't read it until Monday; we'll talk about it then.' I suppose it was one last desperate try; maybe he thought he'd have better luck and Monday would never happen.

The story was 'The Meeting', a marvellous tale set back in 1910 about two well-off young men who quarrel over cards and fight a duel with knives in which one of them dies. At the same time, on the fantastic side, the story is about the secret life of the weapons the men had chosen. I found it remarkably polished, and the draft contained only a couple of minor flaws. One was that in the dark, in a house without electric light, two characters begin studying a cabinet that houses a collection of old knives.

'That's easy,' Borges said as we worked out the translation. 'We'll have one of them light a lamp.' And on the spot, in English, he dictated a line to correct the lapse. My diary entries record that on 3 June I worked very late typing up 'The Meeting' for the *New Yorker*, and that at the library the next evening Borges and I translated the bits of new material into Spanish and inserted them into a set of galley proofs that we then delivered to *La Prensa*, where Peyrou gave each of us a copy of his latest novel *El hijo rechazado*.

Within three weeks we heard from Robert Henderson at the *New Yorker* that they were taking 'The Meeting', and the news had a dramatic effect on Borges. In fact, nothing could have done more just then to send his confidence soaring. In July, on the seventeenth and eighteenth, I read page proofs of *Elogio de la sombra* to him, then read through them a second time alone. I corrected fresh proofs on the twenty-eighth. The book was published to great acclaim in August, on Borges's seventieth birthday. Two days earlier, on the evening of the twenty-second, Emecé gave the book an extravagant send-off on a stage in the Galería Van Riel, where one Dr E. Molina Mascías (whoever he was) spoke at some length, and the '*primera actriz*' (whatever that means) María Rosa Gallo and the '*primeros actores*' (ditto) Enrique Fava and Luis Medina Castro read a large number of the poems. The place was packed out and a bit of a circus. On the copy of the book he gave me the day before, Borges had written, '*Al colaborador, al amigo, al promesso* sposo', for in a few days' time I was to be married. On the Sunday, his birthday, Elsa threw a little party at home with a cake iced in blue and white in the shape and colours of the book itself. You could even read the title on it. It was not at all Borges's style, but he was nonetheless radiant. The next day was the wedding, with Elsa and Borges as the official witnesses at the registry office, and with her sister Alicia Ibarra and cousin Olga and Teddy Paz as extras. Poor Elsa, she was obliged to throw a second party in two days – this one for the *promessi sposi*. Silvina Ocampo and Manuel Puig were there; so was *Elogio de la sombra* – not the book but the cake, or, rather, what was left of it. Plus the wedding cake. By then, though, quite sensibly, Borges had had enough and did not attend. Instead, he went to work at the library.

After that, it all became a whirlwind. In October, two days before 'El encuentro' appeared in *La Prensa*, Borges finished another new story, the one called 'Rosendo's Tale' in English; the day we completed the translation of it we delivered the original to *La Nación*. Now the work found its way into my hands as soon as he finished it. In November came 'The Unworthy Friend', which we took with us to translate in the United States while Borges was lecturing at Oklahoma and where we gave readings and talks at a number of other universities. 'Juan Muraña', the story he had told me about the year before on the very spot where it was set, was finished in mid-January 1970. There was no stopping him now. 'The Duel' came next, but before he put the finishing touches to it he began dictating 'The End of the Duel'. He had long since known he was doing the impossible – writing a new book of stories. On 3 March he finished 'Guayaquil' and on the fifth began 'Doctor Brodie's Report'. The day he finished 'Brodie' he began 'The Gospel According to Mark', completing the first draft of it in under a week. The only hiccup came when he had reached the eight mark. By then he was so anxious to see the collection in print that he ran out of patience. Not of stories, thank goodness, but of patience. He had another three in mind but he simply couldn't wait. As the completed stories were very short, a book of them would have come to no more than seventy pages, and I considered that a mistake. He had been invoking Kipling and the *Plain Tales from the Hills* as a kind of model for his brevity; I pointed out, however, that *Plain Tales* ran to over three hundred pages and contained forty stories. It was no use; he was going to see Frías to tell him he wanted to publish a book of eight stories. And off he went.

I picked up the phone, got Frías, and explained the situation. 'Say no to him,' I told the publisher. 'Tell him he's got to write at least three more. They're there in his head but he's just being lazy.'

Frías saw that I was right. Borges came back and told me that Emecé wanted another three stories. To his credit, he didn't sulk over the news for even a second. Sulking, like self-pity, was never one of Borges's traits. Instead, he immediately set to work writing the three required stories, probably counting his blessings that he had three more stories to tell. I never told him about my intervention. We set about rereading and ordering the book-length typescript in mid-April, a week later he turned it in, and *El informe de Brodie* was published early in August. By any standard, it was a remarkable achievement; by his own, it was nothing short of a miracle. After nine years without writing a book, he had now, within twelve months, written two.

Like Turner, a painter he admired, Borges in his old age also set out to fashion something new, freer, more personal. In many ways he succeeded; undeniably, the prose of his late work is less cluttered and more responsible. He felt that at last he had found his voice. Six more volumes of poetry were to follow *In Praise of Darkness*; seventeen more short stories followed *Doctor Brodie's Report*.

'I no longer regard happiness as unattainable,' he said bravely on reaching seventy-one.

That year, there were no celebrations when the book came out, and certainly there was no cake. Somewhat sadly, circumstances had changed.

There are among my papers two spiral-bound notebooks with ruled pages, workbooks I called them, in which I took down from his dictation on sixty-four recto leaves the story of Borges's life. As far as I am aware, this autobiography is the single most extensive piece of writing Borges ever committed to paper. Like much else that we did, it too seems to have been born of a series of accidents or obstacles – unforeseen and unforeseeable events that somehow or other, uncannily, we kept turning to advantage.

With *The Book of Imaginary Beings* in print and a number of the recent stories and poems beginning to appear in American magazines, Borges and I itched for a chance to present in our own versions a selection of his older stories, the ones on which his fame rested. Of course, we would have preferred to translate the seventeen stories of his best book, *El Aleph*, written in the very rich period between 1945 and 1953, but a competing publisher, who claimed rights to about half these tales, prevented us from doing so. Our own publisher, however, the understanding and very accommodating Jack Macrae, was not averse to obliging us. So by begging, borrowing, and nearly stealing – that is, given the chance, we would have stolen – Borges and I were able to map out the volume that eventually appeared in the autumn of 1970 as *The Aleph and Other Stories 1933–1969*.

The exercise in autobiography had twofold roots. The first of them was in the vexing problem just described, when Borges was denied the right to determine the form and fate of his own work. As our compromise volume took shape, I grew ever more convinced that it needed something in addition to our spanking-new translations if we were to avoid hoodwinking the public with yet another anthology of Borges's work.

The second part of these roots and of the story is a happier affair and even funny. At the University of Oklahoma, several months earlier, I had been able to prevail upon Borges – not without great difficulty – to conclude his set of six lectures on Argentine literature by talking about himself. But on the afternoon of that final lecture he was in a blue funk. He had never before spoken about his own work publicly – it would never have occurred to him to indulge in such a pointless, immodest activity – and it was late in the day, and why on earth, and he simply was not going to be able to go through with it, etc. I saw I had a full-scale panic on my hands. By some strange chemistry, however, his panics always managed to turn the blood in my veins to iced water. It was a partnership, after all, and one of us had to be steady at all times. After our customary afternoon naps – his sleepless and unrefreshing, he claimed – I could see how pent up he was, so I suggested a walk. Our hotel stood about three-quarters of a mile from the campus on what seemed to be the edge of Norman, Oklahoma, where it occupied the corner of a perfectly square block. Arm in arm, Borges and I slowly circumnavigated that block. Once.

'Just remember your Dickens,' I told him. Twice.

'*David Copperfield*,' I told him, '"I was born on a Friday, at twelve o'clock at night."' And three times.

'Nothing fancy, now. You're telling a story, that's all there is to it.'

Every once in a while, Borges's lips began to move. 'I was born in Buenos Aires, in 1899,' he mumbled.

'That's the hang of it,' I said.

He was unconvinced. I couldn't tell him, but so was I.

Of course, he did marvellously, his audience loved it, and our Oklahoma sponsors, Lowell Dunham and Ivar Ivask, were duly pleased. Three months later in Buenos Aires, recalling the little triumph, I had a brainstorm and asked them at Norman to provide us with a transcript of the talk. I wrote to Macrae to tell him that we'd hit on an idea to beef up the book: we would add to it Borges's story of his own life, written directly in English. The lecture, I knew, would come to around twenty pages; I figured that with a few days' work we'd be able to flesh it out to thirty. So carried away was I that somewhere along the line I promised Jack we'd provide the book with a kind of appendix as well, also to be written in English, in the form of commentaries on each of the book's twenty stories. I knew that readers were having difficulty with Borges; worse, I knew that the universities kept him swathed in unnecessary mystery. At the same time, since his stories were really all about himself, his various guises, and dimensions of his thought, what better setting for them by way of introduction than the story of his life?

The pages from Oklahoma reached us sometime in April 1970. By then, we had most of the stories translated and seemed to be on target. But reading the transcript of the lecture, my heart dropped down into my shoes. The talk started out like *David Copperfield*, all right, but it soon went jumping all over the place without order or logic. Sick with worry, I explained the predicament to Borges, for some reason or other fearing a negative response on his part. Instead, undaunted, and paraphrasing one of his favourite authors – English and nineteenth century, of course – he said, 'Fling it aside and be free! We'll start again from scratch.'

We did. On 21 April, the day after the typescript of *El informe de Brodie* went off to Emecé, we pitched in. That first day I took down five pages. I was prepared this time. I made us outline the material beforehand, breaking his life down into manageable chunks, chapters, of which we ended up with five. I made him stick to that outline. 'No, no, don't jump ahead to your mother; let's get it all down about your father and his family first and then we'll tackle her.' It went like that. The next day, I took down five more pages; the day after that, six. At this rate, it was going to come out longer than hoped for, which was all to the good. And better than anything, it looked like being a piece of cake.

On the fourth day, there was a flood of visitors to see Borges at the library and he had a lecture to give at seven o'clock. 'No work done,' says the diary entry. The following week started with permission coming from Grove Press to allow us to make new translations of two vital stories, so we immediately tackled them, since it would permit Macrae to send a good portion of the typescript to the printer while Borges and I worked on. But alas! it was not to be so simple. What with the two translations to get out, a steady stream of visitors from abroad plaguing me, and Borges giving lectures on what seemed every other night, we got not one jot further on the story of his life until 16 May. That day we were down to three and a half pages, and it was not much good.

The fact of the matter was that Borges's mind was on something else. It was at this point that he said to me, 'I've committed what seems to me now an unaccountable mistake, a huge mistake. A quite unexplainable and mysterious mistake.'

He was, of course, referring to his rocky marriage to Elsa, and he was in a pit of despair. It was significant that 16 May was a Saturday. We hadn't worked together on weekends for a very long time, yet here we were once more at the National Library. And it was not because of our deadline with Macrae – it was because Borges could no longer bear life at home. The marriage was not three years old. My diary records that on two days that week Borges had been too distraught for us even to attempt any work. What he needed was to talk about his private life, a thing that was so completely unlike him it only drove home to me the depths of his misery. Most of what he told me I already knew. He poured it out; I listened.

That Saturday was another turning point, for in the afternoon I invited a friend of ours, a lawyer from Córdoba who was in town that week, to tea at the Molino, the big old-fashioned *confitería* by the Congress that he was fond of. Two days later, he and I and Borges went to consult a friend of mine, a local lawyer. Between these two legal minds a bleak picture was painted. For starters, there was no divorce as such under Argentine law – only a form of legal separation that everyone referred to as divorce and that was as effective as any divorce but that did not allow for remarriage.

The next six weeks were an agony. As far as I could, I carried on with the autobiography by myself, typing up whatever dictation we had completed, doing the necessary background research, and checking facts and dates. One Saturday we actually managed to revise half the first chapter. But the next was devoted to drawing up a list of Borges's marital grievances for the Córdoba lawyer. It was not until 28 May that the opening chapter was finished; not until 9 June that we had rewritten the second. We had begun working Sundays now too. But the trouble was that in addition to the delicate, surreptitious work on the legal front – endless meetings with a team of lawyers, countless errands and researching on their behalf – at one and the same time we had too many other matters clamouring for our attention. There were the proofsheets of *El informe de Brodie* to read. That stole three or so days' time, and on the heels of that four more days were lost when we had to produce, in English, a thousand-word introduction to an encyclopaedia article for Grolier, the New York publisher, which was at least a year overdue. Macrae, getting understandably nervous, wanted to publish the stories without any of the new material, but I lied through my teeth and wrote to him that all was coming along fine. It was. What I failed to say was fine – but at a snail's pace.

Meanwhile, I sent the first chapter of the auto-biography to Henderson at the *New Yorker*, asking whether he thought they might be able to use it. He replied at once to say that if the rest were as good, yes. The entire week of 15 June is blank in my diary with only an explanatory scribble, 'no work on auto. essay this week. Spent most of time preparing the divorce.' The next month started out with blank pages as well.

D-Day was 7 July 1970. Only it was not an inva-sion but a getaway. That chill, grey winter's morn-ing – as part of our elaborately hatched plan – I lay in wait for Borges in the doorway of the National Library, and the moment he arrived I leapt into his taxi and off we sped for the intown airport. Borges, a trembling leaf and utterly exhausted after a sleepless night, confessed that his greatest fear had been that he might blurt the whole thing out to Elsa at any moment. Hugo Santiago, the film-maker, who was in on the plot, and my wife were there at the flight counter with a pair of single tickets to Córdoba for Borges and me, where the lawyer had booked us into a hotel only we two knew the name of. Like good conspirators, we allowed no one knowledge of the whole plan. That way, no lies needed to be told, nor could anything be given away. Doña Leonor, Borges's ninety-four-year-old mother, who was punctilious in her rectitude, feared that Elsa would be quick to ring her for information, and while Leonor wanted to be able to say in truth that she did not know her son's whereabouts, still she was anxious to be able to reach him if necessary. That was easy. I gave her a telephone number on a slip of paper in a sealed envelope and had her watch me secrete it in a drawer of her desk.

Bad weather delayed our flight, and a jittery Borges thought the jig was up. Santiago and I did our best to put him at ease, laughing at our own feeble attempts at gallows humour, but it was nervous laughter and both of us, I know, were quaking in our boots. Eventually, by twelve o'clock, our plane took off.

We holed up for a whole week, first in Córdoba, then in Coronel Pringles, where, after a daylong drive across the pampa, we barely arrived in time for a lecture Borges was to deliver on the subject of the Indian raids and the conquest of the desert – meaning the conquest of the Indians – of the previous century. Borges put on a brave face, stubbornly insisting that he was fit to travel these enormous distances, fit to engage in public speaking, but he was on the edge of nervous collapse. The next day his spirits picked up when he could show me the town of Coronel Suárez, some seventy-five kilometres away, named after his great-grandfather. We drove there in caravan with the mayor and other town officials of Pringles, to be met by their counterparts in Suárez, where a splendid midday banquet was laid on for us all. I sat next to the priest, a jolly fellow who, when I told him my religion was *nada*, nothing, made a rather good pun, retorting, '*Nada, nada y nunca se ahoga*' – swim, swim, and never drown. Borges, who hated puns, pronounced this one first-rate.

Eventually, we got to our destination, Pardo, where we stayed in the old dusky-rose house belonging to Bioy Casares, the one that figures in the opening of Borges's story 'The South'. Eventually, we got back to the autobiography too. In fact, by sheer coincidence, it was at Pardo that we reached the point in his life when Borges met Bioy, and we wrote those pages of the story before crackling eucalyptus fires laid on by Bioy's steward. Eventually, we finished the autobiography, not there, nor back in Buenos Aires even, but in the town of Tres Arroyos, again in the far south of the province. Borges had been invited to lecture on the poet Almafuerte. It was 29 July. In a room in the Parque Hotel, Borges lay stretched out on a single bed while I sat on the edge of another, a cleared bedside table between us as my desk, taking down the last words of his dictation. They were not the fine words that come at the end of the finished essay but emendations and additions to the conclusion of the previous paragraph, in which he speaks of longing to write, under a pen name, a merciless tirade against himself. 'Ah, the unvarnished truths I harbour!'

The next week, back home, galley proofs of *The*

Aleph and Other Stories arrived; the week after, the *New Yorker*'s cable saying they were taking the autobiography as a Profile. That same day, 12 August, Borges finished the final draft of his long story 'El Congreso', and together we finished the last two commentaries and our foreword to the book for Macrae. In my diary, there is no mention that the next day I posted the material off, but I must have. Instead, my mind was already on something else. The abstemious entry reads only, 'Errands for Brazil trip.' For it was just then, when he needed it, that the highly remunerative Matarazzo prize had been awarded to Borges for his life's work.

'Here in Argentina,' Borges had told me on my very first morning in Buenos Aires, 'friendship is perhaps more important than love.'

II

II

Borges and His Interpreters

For the most part, explanations of Jorge Luis Borges's work have been more complicated than Borges's work itself. Employing unpronounceable terminology, sometimes even inventing it, these interpretations usually map out elaborate systems whose outline the author, the most haphazard of men, never had the patience or curiosity to follow. Borges had no system, no programme, no grand scheme, and he tells us so twice over in one of his forewords. 'I lay no claim to any particular theories', he wrote in *In Praise of Darkness*, and added, 'I am skeptical of aesthetic theories. They are generally little more than useless abstractions....' He had what he called dreams – by which he meant daydreams. Whim, caprice, and daydreams guided him, even in his private life. So whimsical was he in his daily conduct, in fact, that once asked why he had signed a contract to provide an encyclopaedia article he had no intention of writing, he replied that he was being badgered, that it was a way of changing the subject, and that – as he was leaving for the Argentine the next day – hopefully the publisher would forget all about it.

Such erraticism, hand in hand with a chronic lack of confidence, even spilled over into the way Borges presented his work to the public. Convinced that each published volume would be his last, he never quite knew what to do with a new story or poem. A glimpse into the tangled web of his bibliography in the twenty or so years from the mid-1930s to the mid-1950s tells the story. Fresh work would find its way unannounced not only into a new edition of an old book but also – still secretly – into one or another impression (or, more accurately, 'reimpression') of that edition. (A case in point is Borges's story 'La intrusa', tucked silently into the back of the 1957 edition of *El Aleph* in its so-called sixth impression, which is dated April 1966.)* Had Borges been systematic, his fiction – in terms of separate volumes – would have been richer by at least another title or two.

Writers on Borges have taken him far more seriously than he took himself. Laughter loomed large in Borges's world, and to him literature was joy. Whenever these things are pointed out to his commentators, inevitably they go all solemn and fall back on

* So much for the *tangled web* of Borges bibliography. At another level, it becomes a *minefield*. The 1957 edition just referred to, while labelled 'first edition' is, in fact, a third edition. Its 'sixth impression', strictly speaking, is a fourth edition. And what of the book's 'eighth impression', two years later, which presents 'La intrusa' (and the reader) with the mysterious gift of an unauthorized epigraph? Uncanny how Borges's own books, like his invented Book of Sand, are capable of endless generative powers.

the unanswerable. Invoking the subconscious, they claim that Borges was never fully aware of what he had created. Worse still, so po-faced are these exegetes that to a man (or woman) they miss the point that Jorge Luis Borges was one of the great comic writers of our time.

So let's be guided straight into the vaunted labyrinth of Jorge Luis Borges, unencumbered by the thicket of critical apparatus that has grown up around his work. There is a line in Byron's *Don Juan* – 'I only say, suppose this supposition' – that comes to our aid. If we place these words at the head of almost any Borges story, the Argentine master is made instantly accessible, more so than by any of the vast unreadable library of books, articles, reviews, and doctoral theses that for years now his work has spawned.

Supposing that something were truly unforgettable, thinks Borges; and he imagines the character and circumstances of Funes, a young Uruguayan who, as the result of a childhood accident, is afflicted with total recall, so that he possesses 'more memories than the rest of mankind since the world began'. Supposing the past could be undone, muses Borges; and he constructs the masterful tale 'The Other Death', in which, forty years after committing a cowardly act in battle, a man dies the kind of death he would have preferred to die. What if, asks Borges, all expression, all language, all poetry could be reduced to a single line or even a single word; and he dreams up two of his most genial tales, 'The Mirror and the Mask' and 'Undr', in which an Irish bard and a Norse skald, respectively, set out in quest of the unfathomable essence of absolute poetry. Or what if, Borges posits, there were a book with an infinite number of pages; and he invents the Book of Sand, a volume in which 'None is the first page, none the last.'

Borges formally commented on a number of his own stories. Twenty of them, in fact. These remarks, written directly in English, appear in a long-out-of-print volume called *The Aleph and Other Stories 1933–1969*. One has only to compare what he said there with what the exegetes have concocted to see how simple and direct Borges was, how far from the inhuman, slightly monstrous literary intelligence he was too frequently made out to be. Having worked with him for a number of years, having lived in Buenos Aires, where I was immersed in his world, having translated ten or so of his books and studied his writing for decades, I find the line from Byron almost magical for the ease with which it lets us into Borges's mind. In the teeth of the mystification, complication, and misconception that the bulk of Borges's commentators have strewn in our path, I view him as an exacting craftsman and as a pure and rather old-fashioned teller of tales – one whose starting point is not 'Once upon a time ...' but rather 'Let us suppose ...' or 'What if ...'

Some years ago, I commented on a book about this

Borges, the story-teller. The volume under scrutiny, I said at the time, was perhaps the the best-written book on Borges to date in English. It managed to be scholarly without too great a reek of the academy. Borges's stories, its author accurately pointed out,

are exemplary, not morally exemplary like the stories once written by Cervantes and others to teach improving lessons in human conduct, but technically exemplary in that they dramatise the rules and procedures of the narrative genre to which they belong....

The book correctly went on to characterize Borges's fiction as 'think pieces', tales about ideas rather than people. The volume contained several chapters of other valuable insights and observations, including one which comprised a perfect discussion of the philosophical basis of so much of Borges's work.

Yet oddly the book was peppered with misconceptions and strange little inaccuracies that turned some of its arguments comic. At one point, to illustrate a particular thesis, the volume cited a four-page tale from Borges's first fictional work, *A Universal History of Infamy*, claiming that the piece was 'loosely derived from the Arabic' and that it was 'one of Borges's earliest inventions'. But the story was not by Borges at all. While indeed a similar tale figures in an Arabian collection, the one borrowed by Borges here was an almost straight transcription from the medieval text of the Spanish infante Don Juan Manuel. As it turned out, Borges deliberately chose the story and put it into his own collection for the simple reason that as narrative – as the kind of imaginative narrative he was to make his hallmark – it was a better piece of work than he was then, in the early 1930s, capable of writing. That, it seems to me, is the point that should have been made.

Elsewhere in the same study, discussing another of the tales from *A Universal History of Infamy*, the author got a more serious detail wrong. Citing a lead given him by an American Borges commentator, Ronald Christ, the author states that Borges's version of the Tichborne claimant story was derived from an account of it in Philip Gosse's *History of Piracy*. It is difficult to comprehend what place the story of the great swindle of Victorian times, involving a noted old Catholic family and the supposed return of their long-lost son, could possibly have in a survey of buccaneers. I once pointed out to Christ that his interpretation had been based not on a reading of Gosse but on an error committed by an Argentine typesetter who, in a reprint of the *Historia universal de la infamia,* misplaced the linotype slug that accurately credits the source of the Tichborne story to the pages of the *Encyclopædia Britannica.* Christ later acknowledged this in print and recounted how a simple printer's error had led to what he called, poking fun at himself, 'inevitable interpretive fictions'.

Some forty pages after first speaking of Gosse in the volume I reviewed, its author made the following full-blown reference to this same story, perpetrating yet another 'inevitable interpretative fiction':

As readers of Borges' story we might ... compare his Tichborne claimant with the original.... By comparison with Gosse, Borges' story is the most blatant of fictions and all the more interesting for being so. He no more wants to imitate Gosse than Bogle [a character in the story] wants to imitate Roger Tichborne. On the other hand, it is Gosse's story that we have to see as the 'reality' from which Borges' translation departs.... The two versions vary in their circumstances, Borges having invented, for his purposes, quite different circumstances from those invented, or selected, by Philip Gosse.

While I was engaged in the translation of *A Universal History of Infamy* back in 1971, Borges made me a gift of several of the books he had used as source material when writing his tales. One of them was the Gosse volume, which had been utilized – quite logically – for a story about Chinese pirates. There is no connection or reference whatever in Gosse to the Tichborne affair, therefore I cannot even begin to speculate on what led the commentator to become so carried away by a text that does not exist. But then how typical of Borges, the sleight-of-hand master of bogus attributions and of texts that go missing, to subsume his interpreters in this way.

The story does not end there. In his notes to a 1998 compendium of Borges's stories, Andrew Hurley – twenty-six years after Christ's confession of error – could still claim in a statement that is a model of unclarity and equivocation that Gosse's history is the source given by Borges, but 'In my view, this attribution is the result of an initial error seized upon by Borges for another of his "plays with sources"; as he subsequently admitted freely, and as many critics have noted, much of this story comes from the *Encyclopædia Britannica*, Eleventh Edition....' So much for Hurley's scholarship and his insight into Borges's mind. So much for the acumen of the Borges estate in specifying that Hurley's compendium be based on a substandard edition of Borges's works. So much for the competence of Borges's Buenos Aires publisher. A mere glance by any of these at the original edition of the work in question would have been enough to correct the typographical error, set the record straight, and bring to an end decades of waffle and absurd supposition. In the preface to one of his story collections, Borges mocked a standard reference work '*dont chaque édition fait regretter la précédente*' – of which each new edition makes you yearn for the previous one. He laughed when we translated the passage and, with a tinge of sadness, added, 'My complete works.'

My point is that these interpreters have been so cowed by Borges that rather than read what is there on the page with a bit of common sense they have instead been overly eager to intellectualize, to construct theories, to pit themselves against Borges in playing a far more complicated game than he ever intended. Blame for this to some extent can be laid to the fact that Borges is often studied in English, in poor translations, without reference to his Argentine roots. English-speaking critics, when they first came across Borges's work in the early 1960s, appeared to believe that he had sprung from nowhere. Because his work drew on all Western (and Eastern) culture, his admirers often branded him a European writer. So did his detractors at home. Paradoxically, these virulent nationalists – because Borges refused to dabble in local colour, because he displayed maverick qualities such as a fondness for irony and subversion, because he thought for himself and was not afraid to speak his mind – could not see his profound roots in Argentine soil.* My greatest discovery when I went to work with Borges in Buenos Aires was to find that his books could not have been written by anyone but an Argentine.

Down the years there has been an uncanny and unholy tendency in academic circles – American ones,

---

* An example of the kind of unpalatable truth that many despised him for making in public would be this pronouncement, dating from 1983: 'Keeping evil hidden away is one of the forms of Argentine hypocrisy. It does not matter that there may be slums all over Buenos Aires; what is troubling is that foreigners see them…. What matters is not reality but appearance.'

in particular – to overinterpret. I suppose this came about for two reasons. One is because the grinders out of doctoral theses do not understand how writers write. As a result of the verbal fireworks perpetrated by James Joyce in *Finnegans Wake*, they erroneously believe that the prose writer's basic unit is the word, when in fact an author works in ideas, pages, paragraphs, or sentences, all guided by cadences – in short, a flow, a sweep, not a dribble. Towards the end of his life, Borges told a London audience that to him literature was made

Not just juggling with words. I try to forget the words and to say what I have to say perhaps not through the words but in spite of the words, and if a book is really good you forget the words.

A second reason for overinterpreting is that the academic, like the politician in office, must perpetuate himself in his position. Therefore, it has been a matter of interpreting or perishing, of putting every word under the microscope and finding the hidden fauna. In Borges exegesis this has often amounted to dwelling on single words and overloading them with significance.

A favourite anecdote about this brand of overloading concerns a private interview I once had with a professor at a Pennsylvania university. He was teaching a Borges story in English and asked me what

the significance of the colour red was on the walls
of a particular building in a certain Borges story. I
imagine he wanted it confirmed that the hue stood
for bloodshed and violence, thus foreshadowing the
conclusion of the tale in question. Perhaps it did,
though I doubt it. (Perhaps it even had a remote political significance, but I doubt that too.) For one
thing, I always noted a concern in Borges not to give
his endings away, a tendency that made him shun
foreshadowing. Not to give their themes away when
he attached epigraphs to at least two of his stories, he
quoted no words but cited only the name, chapter,
and verse of his sources.

Chagrined and disbelieving, my professor walked
away when I told him that what Borges had described was the actual colour of an actual structure,
one that belonged to his friend Adolfo Bioy Casares.*
I knew the place, for once – when Borges was having
marital difficulties – he and I had holed up there for
a few days. The building, as was common in those
parts, was simply red. I never got the chance to tell
the professor that the colour, a traditional one, was

---

* The colour – a scarlet faded to pink, or, in effect, a dusky pink –
also figures earlier in the story in question. Here the pink of a house
is described as having once been crimson. In 1928 – in a short piece
he re-used in 1946 – Borges, singling out a dusky-rose wall, went on
to say that 'There is probably no better way of representing fondness
than by that particular dusky pink.' I link his evocation of this colour
with my remarks about Borges's 'South' as an emblem of the Argentine past – of his personal view of that past. See pp. 83–4.

originally derived from lime wash mixed with the blood of a bull. In fact, in his Spanish, Borges did not employ the general word for red but mentioned a certain vivid red known in the Argentine as *punzó*. The political comment, if there was one, concerns the use of this particular word. Borges qualified it with a nicely observed detail and said that the place had *once* been this shade of red but that 'to its benefit the years had softened that vivid colour.' The colour, I prefer to believe, reflects a fact of daily life on the Argentine pampa – as does the fact that the building needed a coat of paint. On two counts, Borges had accurately depicted the structure. Anything else he would probably have looked on as mere cleverness. For the reader of Borges, there is no need to ignore what is before one's eyes and look for the far-fetched.

When it becomes difficult to trust that a wall is red because it is red because it is red, we must question the limits of legitimate interpretation. Common sense should apply, just as in rabbinical exegesis, as a safeguard against esoteric and misleading interpretation, the primary meaning of language takes precedence. Writers are admired for pinning down an object, a mood, the ineffable, with precision. Borges's prose, largely modelled on writers like Stevenson, Wells, and Chesterton, is realistic and as such it is full of sharp definition. Alas, the diction and mistakes of poor translations of Borges into English blur his prose

and make it the victim of distortion born of ignorance. A common enough meteorological phenomenon, the red ring around the moon that forecasts
rain, comes out in one story as 'the crimson circle
around the moon presaged rain.' In another, a small
kettle used to brew maté – an everyday household
utensil on the River Plate – is transmogrified into a
'soup cauldron'. In another, 'a growth of tall reeds',
a common detail of the Argentine countryside, is
bludgeoned into 'a field covered in dried-out straw'.
(While Borges was fascinated by the exotic in alien
cultures, paradoxically he hated exotic descriptions
of life in his own country.) In a fourth, the word
jineta, which in Spanish means 'shoulder braid'
or 'insignia', is misread for the word *jinetes*, which
means 'horsemen' or 'riders'. In the tale, the hero, a
policeman who is about to take the side of the man
he is hunting down, is troubled over his rank and
uniform – in other words, over his shoulder braid,
the emblem of his authority. The translation in
question has him troubled about 'the other cavalry-
men'. The wonder was, Borges remarked, that the
translator had not taken *jinetas* for the feminine of
jinetes and had the hero troubled about 'the Ama-
zons'.

Another stock-in-trade of many interpreters has
been the clever game of combing words for double
meanings. Not satisfied that the Spanish word *fuentes*
means only 'fountains' in a particular instance, one

study tells us that the word is more helpfully translated into English as 'sources', which is a second Spanish meaning of the word. I grow impatient with this. Borges was writing about public fountains in a place like Trafalgar Square. I do not believe we find 'sources' in London squares. *Fuente* in Spanish can also meaning a serving dish. Why hadn't that been thrown in for good measure? I am reminded of one translator of a Borges poem who went in for such surrealism when, translating the Spanish word *cascos*, he opted for 'helmets' instead of 'hoofs'. The poem was about horses. Perhaps in Hieronymus Bosch horses have helmets, but in Borges, on the Argentine pampa, they have hoofs. In this case, the translator – a Latin American and at the time a professor at yet another Pennsylvania university – astonished Borges with his arrogance. The man read his version one day to an audience that included Borges. Afterwards, Borges took him aside and said, 'Look here, *cascos* is "hoofs".' That evening, the man read the poem out again at another public gathering. Of course, the word had not been changed.

Even worse are those interpreters who look for and of course find bilingual puns in Borges. One once extracted the colour 'red' from the Spanish word *enredadera*, which means – plain and simple – a vine or creeper. Are we supposed to stand in awe and applaud such cleverness? Borges made no secret of his abhorrence of monolingual, let alone bilingual, puns.

In the end, the explanations – the best of them, that is – simply cease to illuminate and begin to stultify. As a poet friend once remarked to me, 'Literature can't be taught. Either you get it or you don't.' So much explaining, then, explains nothing, and if we want to understand Borges we must allow his prose to speak for itself. Look at the openings of the stories 'The Other' and 'Ulrike' from his last full set of stories, *The Book of Sand*. 'The Other' begins:

It was in Cambridge, back in February 1969, that the event took place. I made no attempt to record it at the time, because, fearing for my mind, my initial aim was to forget it. Now, some years later, I feel that if I commit it to paper others will read it as a story and, I hope, one day it will become a story for me as well. I know it was horrifying while it lasted – and even more so during the sleepless nights that followed – but this does not mean that an account of it will necessarily move anyone else.

'Ulrike' begins:

My story will be true to reality or, in any case, to my personal memory of reality, which amounts to the same thing. The events took place only a short time ago, but I know that literary habit is also the habit of adding circumstantial details and of underlining high points. I want to give an account of my meeting with Ulrike (I never knew her surname and perhaps never shall) in the city of York. The narrative will encompass one night and a morning.

In my own heretical opinion, this, as prose, was the best and most responsible that Borges ever wrote. It is more immediate, spare, and direct than ever, and it must be remembered that, where concision is concerned, Borges always achieved more in one or two pages than any other writer of our age.

Jorge Luis Borges was a product of another era, of a time when people read books for the sheer enjoyment of them and for the genuine ideas and talk that they stimulated. He has described how as a young man circles of friends, including his father and his father's friends, would meet in all-night sessions to discuss literature and philosophy on a particular evening at a particular café once each week. These Buenos Aires literary men were all amateurs in the true sense of the word. As a writer, especially as a critic, Borges retained something of the amateur until his final days. I think this is the real meaning behind his claim, which surprises so many, that he was first a reader, then a poet, then a story writer. It has never ceased to amuse me, then, that a man who never earned a university degree or was ever a university student should have come to be so assiduously studied in academic circles. It amused Borges too. He often told me he feared that at any moment the bubble would burst and that he would be found out – found somehow to be wanting.

How did Borges react to all this overinterpretation? Well, politely, graciously. On numerous occasions I heard his stock reply to anyone who laid it on the line and told him what some piece of work of his was really about. Borges always smiled, humbly and sweetly, and 'Ah, thank you!' would come his ambiguous put-down. 'You have enriched my work!'

Borges at Play: The Self and the Selves

For Francis Spencer

Philosophy, beginning in wonder, is able to fancy everything different from what it is.

–William James

In a tale that comes down to us from before 300 BC, Chuang Tzu dreamed he was a butterfly and on waking did not know whether he was a man who had dreamed he was a butterfly or a butterfly who now dreamed he was a man.

The story, a favourite of Borges's, was one he also made emblematic. In a tale of his own, a man dreams a disciple into being and at the end understands 'that he, too, was an appearance, that someone else was dreaming him.'

Illusion and reality; the real and the imaginary. Borges, in his inimitable brand of fiction, made a particular mark by playing verbal games with philosophical concepts, some of which touched on mystical or hermetic ideas. What much of his writing attempted – as he once put it – was to turn his own perplexities 'and that respected system of perplexities we call philosophy into the forms of literature.'

I want to explore one of these philosophical themes – the idea of the self or selves in Borges – and follow it in its various aspects through a handful of his stories and poems and in one or two of his readings of other writers. There was no systematic approach to the dilemma of identity in Borges, no step-by-step development of the riddle; rather, his path was a problematic, disjointed journey from multiplicity to wholeness. A good deal of his exploration of the subject – in the form of essays, stories, and prose poems, or parables – took place in a concentrated period during the late 1940s and early 1950s, when several crises in Borges's life converged. The most general statement of the theme is to be found in *The Book of Imaginary Beings*, in the article on 'The Double'. The page reads:

Suggested or stimulated by reflections in mirrors and in water and by twins, the idea of the Double is common to many countries. It is likely that sentences such as *A friend is another self* by Pythagoras or the Platonic *Know thyself* were inspired by it. In Germany this Double is called *Doppelgänger*, which means 'double walker'. In Scotland there is the fetch, which comes to fetch a man to bring him to his death; there is also the Scottish word wraith for an apparition thought to be seen by a person in his exact image just before death. To meet oneself is, therefore, ominous. The tragic ballad 'Ticonderoga' by Robert Louis Stevenson tells of a legend on this theme. There is also the strange picture by Rossetti ('How They Met Themselves') in which two lovers come upon themselves in the dusky gloom of a wood. We may also cite examples from Hawthorne ('Howe's Masquerade'), Dostoyevsky, Alfred de Musset, James ('The Jolly Corner'), Kleist, Chesterton ('The Mirror of Madmen'), and Hearn (*Some Chinese Ghosts*).

The ancient Egyptians believed that the Double, the *ka*, was a man's exact counterpart, having his same walk and his same dress. Not only men, but gods and beasts, stones and trees, chairs and knives had their *ka*, which was invisible except to certain priests who could see the Doubles of the gods and were granted by them a knowledge of things past and things to come.

To the Jews the appearance of one's Double was not an omen of imminent death. On the contrary, it was proof of having attained prophetic powers. This is how it is explained by Gershom Scholem. A legend recorded in the Talmud tells the story of a man who, in search of God, met himself.

In the story 'William Wilson' by Poe, the Double is the hero's conscience. He kills it and dies. In a similar way, Dorian Gray in Wilde's novel stabs his portrait and meets his death. In Yeats's poems the Double is our other side, our opposite, the one who complements us, the one we are not nor will ever become.

Plutarch writes that the Greeks gave the name *other self* to a king's ambassador.

We have several ideas here. There is the notion of the double as another side, or opposite, of ourselves.

In its broadest application, this embraces the view of the writer as fantasist, as a man taking on and playing out other roles – something akin to Yeats's 'Mask' and Pound's 'personae'. In Borges, the most obvious example of such role playing is found in his fascination with knives and with knife fights, a passion that made its first appearance in a 1927 sketch and went on in a series of stories and poems right to the end of his long life. In most of this work his participation in the events he narrates was little more than vicarious. No one in his parade of knife wielders is the historical Borges, but what we have in them instead is a dim representation of something Borges would have liked to have been. In one knife story, however – 'The South', written in 1953 – the projection is clearly of an alter ego. For some years Borges spoke of the story as perhaps his best.

In the tale, Juan Dahlmann, a municipal librarian and grandson on one side of his family of German Protestant immigrants, comes home to his Buenos Aires apartment one night in February 1939, bearing under his arm a copy of the Gustav Weil translation of the Thousand and One Nights. So eager is Dahlmann to look into his acquisition that he does not bother waiting for the lift to descend but hastily takes to the stairs. He has an accident. On the stairway he brushes into the corner of a freshly painted casement window that has carelessly been left open. The resulting scalp wound lands him in the hospital with blood poisoning, and for eight days, which are like eight centuries, he hangs between life and death, racked with fever and nightmares that are exacerbated by illustrations from the pages of the Thousand and One Nights. Transferred to another hospital, he undergoes surgery. In the next few days, as he makes his recovery,

Dahlmann despised every last bit of himself; he despised who he was, his bodily necessities, his humiliation, the beard that bristled on his face. The treatment of his wound, which was very painful, he bore stoically, but when his doctor told him that he had nearly died of septicemia, Dahlmann, pitying himself for what he had been through, burst into tears.

Now the story shifts. For his convalescence, Dahlmann decides to go to the small ranch to the south of Buenos Aires that he has managed to salvage from more extensive lands once owned by his Argentine forebears. On the way to the station, he reflects, nostalgically, that the south − of his city, of his country − stands for an older world and an older order, for a purely Argentine past. On the train Dahlmann takes out the copy of the Thousand and One Nights. Looking through the window, he notes with pleasure the various elements of the landscape, among them

trees and crops that he would not have been able to name, for his direct knowledge of the countryside was somewhat inferior to his sentimental and literary knowledge of it.

For some reason or other, explained by a guard but which Dahlmann does not understand, the train cannot stop at his customary station, and he must get off earlier at a place he does not recognize – a kind of platform with a shed in the middle of the boundless plain. He makes his way to a small inn, where he sits down to dine while awaiting transport to his ranch. While Dahlmann eats, some half-drunk hoodlums at another table begin pelting him with bits of bread. Dahlmann tries to ignore this and, as he has finished his meal anyway, is about to leave when the owner of the place, addressing him by name, tells him not to pay attention to the boys, who have been drinking. Realizing now that he is known, Dahlmann feels the insult both to him and to his name. He approaches the young men and asks them what they want. One of them erupts into foul language and, whipping out a knife, invites Dahlmann to fight with him. It is noticed that Dahlmann is unarmed, and someone throws a knife at his feet. At this point,

It was as though the South had decided that Dahlmann should accept the challenge. He bent over to pick up the knife and felt two things. First, that this almost instinctive action bound him to fight. Second, that in his clumsy hand the weapon would not serve to defend him but only to justify his being killed.

The two men move to the door. The story comes to its climax.

Crossing the threshold, Dahlmann felt that to die in a knife fight under the open sky and on his feet would have been, that first night in the hospital, when they stuck him with the needle, a liberation, a happiness, a festivity. He felt that if he had been able then to choose or dream his own death, this is the death he would have chosen or dreamed.

To here the story has been told in the past tense. It now concludes with this one-sentence paragraph in the present:

Dahlmann clutches the knife, which he may not know how to handle, and steps out onto the plain.

Borges's immigrant forebears were English, not German, but all the other details and all the essential facts at the opening of 'The South' came out of his own personal history and direct experience. Borges had been a municipal librarian, his ancestry on one side was Protestant, and everything about the accident and cure – even its date, 1939, when an identical misfortune befell him – was autobiographical. So was the nice detail of bibliophily, for Borges had admired and collected the Arabian Nights, and he even wrote about its German translators – including Weil. The south as an emblem of the Argentine past – and by this Borges did not mean Patagonia; he meant both the south side of Buenos Aires and the south of the province of Buenos Aires – and the mystique of this south were very much Borges's dearly held private views. This south that he turned into myth represented his childhood, a link with his forebears and what seemed to him – remember, the story was written in 1953, two years before Perón was routed – the less abysmal days of a pre-Peronist Argentina.

Where the action in the story shifts, however, and Dahlmann rides the train south, the events are purely fictional, though certain of the details are not. The description of Dahlmann's ranch in Flores fits that of the ranch of Borges's old friend Adolfo Bioy Casares, which is also in Flores. Even the remark that Dahlmann's knowledge of the countryside tended to the literary was autobiographical. Elsewhere, in speaking of his first boyhood experiences of the pampa, Borges said, 'I have always come to things after coming to books.' Borges himself was never involved in a knife fight; the Dahlmann at the climax of the story is Borges engaged in wishful thinking. Many times Borges expressed to me his longing for an end exactly like the one we expect for Dahlmann. Alas, when death eventually came to him, Borges died of cancer, weak, frail, bedridden, and – perhaps most poignant of all – in Geneva, far from his idealized *sur*. What he had written in 'The South', then, was a scenario of his own ideal end.

Of the fifty or so short stories Borges wrote, knives figure prominently in about ten of them and peripherally in at least three others. For a man who spent the largest portion of his eighty-seven years with his nose in a book, for a man who was a librarian by profession, for an author of the most bookish books in all twentieth-century literature – if not of all time – I think we can safely agree that this is a large order of bloodletting and gore. Why, we ask ourselves, did this most gentle and humane of men wish to dream himself into Juan Dahlmann's shoes and meet such a violent end? The answer, I think, is to be found in Borges's autobiography. Here we learn that Borges's maternal great-grandfather, as a captain at the age of twenty-four, led a famous cavalry charge and turned the tide in one of the last battles of the South American wars of independence; this was Isidoro Suárez, and he ended as a colonel. Another remoter ancestor, a prominent public figure and one of the nation's founding fathers, was hunted down and killed in an 1829 civil war; this was Francisco de Laprida, the protagonist of Borges's 'Conjectural Poem'. One of Borges's grandfathers, Isidoro Acevedo, took part in yet other civil wars of the 1860s and 1880s. Borges's other grandfather, Francisco Borges, was a colonel who commanded outposts in the wars against the Indians during the early 1870s and who, in 1874, died in battle in rather complicated and bizarre circumstances. About to be reduced to ignominy after having backed the wrong side in a revolution, Colonel Borges, wrapped in a white poncho, rode out on a white horse towards the enemy lines. Two bullets, fired by the first Remingtons to be used in the Argentine, cut him down, and he died two days later – out in the open, with his boots on. Just as, presumably, Juan Dahlmann was to do sixty-five years later. 'So,' wrote Borges with typical self-irony, 'on both sides of my family, I have military forebears; this may account for my yearning after that epic destiny which my gods denied me, no doubt wisely.' And he goes on:

… I spent a great deal of my boyhood indoors. Having no childhood friends, my sister and I invented two imaginary companions, named, for some reason or other, Quilos and The Windmill. (When they finally bored us, we told our mother that they had died.) I was always very nearsighted and wore glasses, and I was rather frail. As most of my people had been soldiers – even my father's brother had been a naval officer – and I knew I would never be, I felt ashamed, quite early, to be a bookish kind of person and not a man of action.

In a sonnet on the death of Colonel Francisco Borges, his grandson wrote:

I leave him on his horse on that evening
In which he rode across the plain to meet
His death, and of all the hours of his fate
May this one, though bitter, go on living.
White horse, white poncho pick a studied way
Over the flat terrain. Ahead, death lurks
Patiently in the barrels of the guns.

Colonel Borges sadly crosses the plain.
What closed on him, the Remingtons' crackle,
What his eye took in, endless grazing land,
Are what he saw and heard his whole life long.
Here was his home – in the thick of battle.
In his epic world, riding on his horse,
I leave him almost untouched by my verse.

Francisco Borges on his horse and Juan Dahl-mann stepping out onto the plain – projections of another self that a myopic, studious Borges could only long for – are Borges's simplest expression of the quandary of self and identity. In the life of one of his literary heroes, Walt Whitman, Borges recognized a similar split. In an essay written in 1947, Borges suggested that

there are two Whitmans: the 'friendly and eloquent savage' of *Leaves of Grass* and the poor writer who invented him.... The latter was chaste, reserved, and somewhat taciturn; the former, outgoing and orgiastic.

In 1969, in the foreword to his translation of *Leaves of Grass*, Borges wrote more explicitly that the hero Whitman created for his poetry had

a two-fold nature: he is the modest journalist Walter Whitman, native of Long Island, [and] at the same time he is the other person that the first man wanted to be and was not – a man of adventure and love, indolent, courageous, carefree, a wanderer throughout America....

The dichotomy was one that a more and more inward-looking Borges came increasingly to pinpoint in his own life. Again, in Emerson, Borges detected an analogous division. Finding an expression of dissatisfaction in Emerson's poem 'Days', Borges maintained that the New Englander 'is repentant of having lived little, of having contented himself with a few experiences and much literature.' In a poem on Emerson, Borges wrote:

He moves through darkening fields as he moves now
Through the memory of the one who writes this down.
He thinks: I have read the essential books
And written others which oblivion
Will not efface. I have been allowed
That which is given mortal man to know.
The whole continent knows my name.
I have not lived. I want to be someone else.

This dissatisfaction, turned completely inward, we will look at in a moment when we come to discuss Borges in terms of a divided self.

Let us consider the idea of the fetch and the wraith. The fetch is a double which comes to take a man to his death; the wraith, an apparition seen by a person in his exact image just before death. In Borges, the two are closely related and are often combined with the notion of self-knowledge. Often their agent is the mirror. Hence, in 'Camden 1892', a sonnet on the death of Walt Whitman, the old poet lies in his bed and

He glances at his face in the exhausted
Mirror. He thinks, without surprise now,
That face is me. One fumbling hand touches
The tangled beard, the devastated mouth.
The end is not far off. His voice declares:
I am almost gone.

Hence, also, in 'May 20, 1928', a poem on the death by suicide of a young Argentine poet:

He will go down to the lavatory. There on the chessboard-patterned floor tiles, water will wash the blood away quite soon. The mirror awaits him.
He will smooth back his hair, adjust his tie ... and try to imagine that the other man – the one in the mirror – performs the actions and that he, the double, repeats them. His hand will not falter at the end. Obediently, magically, he will have pressed the weapon to his head.

Here Borges enriches the theme, but still there is no step towards resolution. In one story, however – 'The Life of Tadeo Isidoro Cruz' – he seems to move closer to an answer through the phenomenon of identification with one's opposite and enemy. Cruz, hunting down an outlaw, comes to discover himself in the other man. Cruz had been born forty-one years before, when his father, a gaucho militiaman, was hunted down and killed in the aftermath of battle. Cruz grows up as a gaucho drover, taking part in cattle drives. On the way back from one such drive to Buenos Aires, taunted by one of his fellows, he lays the man out with a knife blow and turns outlaw. Captured, he is made to serve in the army, where he fights in several skirmishes with Indians. Later, he settles down and becomes the local police sergeant. It is in this role that Cruz, somewhere in the vicinity of where his father was killed years before, is leading a search party to capture an army deserter who has killed two men. What lay in wait for Cruz, Borges wrote,

was a night of stark illumination – the night in which at last he glimpsed his own face, the night in which at last he heard his name…. Any life, no matter how long or complex it may be, is made up essentially *of a single moment* – the moment in which a man finds out, once and for all, who he is…. To Tadeo Isidoro Cruz, who did not know how to read, this revelation was not given by a book; it was in a manhunt and in the man he was hunting that he learned who he was.

It is night. The deserter is tracked to a clump of tall reeds, where he may be asleep or lying in wait. Cruz and his men move forward stealthily. The hunted man springs out and fights them, savagely wounding or killing a number of Cruz's troops. Cruz recognizes the spot as the place where his father met his end and where he had been born; then, while fighting in the dark, he

began to understand. He understood that one destiny is no better than another, but that every man must obey what is within him. He understood that his shoulder braid and his uniform were now in his way. He understood that his real destiny was as a lone wolf, not a gregarious dog. He understood that the other man was himself. Day dawned over the boundless plain. Cruz threw down his kepi, called out that he would not be party to the crime of killing a brave man, and began fighting against his own soldiers, shoulder to shoulder with Martín Fierro, the deserter.

At the heart of Borges's 'Conjectural Poem' is another hunted man who, just before his death, comes to find out who he is. The protagonist this time is the Francisco de Laprida referred to earlier. Fleeing for his life, again in the aftermath of a lost battle, Laprida is pursued by a band of gaucho militia. It is night, and he is making his way along a kind of embankment with marshes on either side. The form of the poem is the dramatic monologue. Laprida thinks to himself:

> I hear the
> hooves of my own hot death riding me down
> with horsemen, frothing muzzles, and lances.

In these last moments before his throat is cut, he reflects on his career as a jurist and one of the signers

of an 1826 constitution – in other words, as a man
who represents civilization rather than the present
barbarism that threatens not only his life but his
life's work and his country's future:

I, who longed to be someone else, to weigh
judgments, to read books, to hand down the law,
will lie in the open out in these swamps;
but a secret joy somehow swells my breast.
I see at last that I am face to face
with my South American destiny.
I was carried to this ruinous hour
by the intricate labyrinth of steps
woven by my days from a day that goes
back to my birth. At last I've discovered
the mysterious key to all my years,
the fate of Francisco de Laprida,
the missing letter, the perfect pattern
that was known to God from the beginning.
In this night's mirror I can comprehend
my unsuspected true face. The circle's
about to close. I wait to let it come.

This time the mirror is not an actual one but stands
for Laprida's last night alive, which has brought him
knowledge of himself. In a later poem, 'In Praise of
Darkness', Borges reflects on his own blindness and
impending death:

From south and east and west and north
roads coming together have led me
to my secret center.

These roads are listed. They are all the men and women Borges had known, all his days and nights, his sleep and dreams – all time, in fact – as well as his reading and other pleasures. Then, closing the poem, he goes on:

Now I can forget them. I reach my center,
my algebra and my key,
my mirror.
Soon I shall know who I am.

At the end of another of Borges's books, *El hacedor* (unfortunately translated into English as *Dreamtigers*; its original title means 'The Maker', a name that Borges thought up in English and translated into Spanish), we read this celebrated passage:

A man sets himself the task of depicting the world. Year after year, he fills a space with images of provinces, kingdoms, mountains, bays, ships, islands, fishes, rooms, instruments, stars, horses, and people. Just before he dies, he discovers that out of this patient labyrinth of lines emerge the features of his own face.

In the 'Conjectural Poem', in 'In Praise of Darkness', and in the tailpiece from *The Maker* – all of which are about the discovery of the self in the face of death – the argument has shifted forward to an identification of the double not in another character but in the hero's own death. Now the circle of projection has closed in on the author himself, and Borges seems to have found a place of 'oneness', a point of identity in and beyond the antagonistic and bewildering multiplicity of his life. He has found, in short, his centre. If we wanted a simple, happy ending to this exploration of Borges and his selves we might be tempted to stop here.

But Borges was not content to rest at this point – not with a mere gallery of outwardly projected characters and alter egos. Instead, in his later work we find the division of self driven inward with a fearful intensity and a narrowing progression. Let us look at three texts – out of chronology, as Borges would no doubt have preferred – in which the selves are not fictional projections but differing aspects of one and the same person.

The progression begins playfully enough in a tale called 'The Other', a purely autobiographical treatment of the theme of the double in the form of a lightly teasing conversation between an older and a younger Borges. The narrator, seated on a bench by the Charles River in Cambridge, Massachusetts, in 1969, is the seventy-year-old Borges; the 'other' is the nineteeeen-year-old, somewhat priggish Borges, who insists that they are sitting by the Rhône, in Geneva, and that the year is 1918. The younger Borges, who registers increasing fear and dismay, takes up an insistent, challenging tone. The plot sets out to determine which of the two is dreaming the other. 'Beneath our conversation', says the older man near the end,

I realized that we were unable to understand each other. We were too similar and too unalike. We were unable to take each other in.... Each of us was a caricature copy of the other.

Next, in 'Borges y yo' – or, as he and I called it in our English version, 'Borges and Myself' – comes this more charged dialogue between the private and the public Borges in what is one of the author's best as well as most famous pages:

It's to the other man, to Borges, that things happen. I walk along the streets of Buenos Aires, stopping now and then – perhaps out of habit – to look at the arch of an old entrance-way or a grillwork gate; of Borges I get news through the mail and glimpse his name among a committee of professors or in a dictionary of biography. I have a taste for hourglasses, maps, eighteenth-century typography, the roots of words, the smell of coffee, and Stevenson's prose; the other man shares these likes, but in a showy way that turns them into stagy mannerisms. It would be an exaggeration to say that we are on bad terms; I live, I let myself live, so that Borges can weave his tales and poems, and those tales and poems are my justification. It is not hard for me to admit that he has managed to write a few worthwhile pages, but these pages cannot save me, perhaps because what is good no longer belongs to anyone – not even the other man – but rather to speech or tradition. In any case, I am fated to become lost once and for all, and only some moment of myself will survive in the other man. Little by little, I have been surrendering to him, even though I have evidence of his stubborn habit of falsification and exaggerating. Spinoza held that all things try to keep on being themselves; a stone wants to be a stone and the tiger, a tiger. I shall remain in Borges, not in myself (if it is so that I am someone), but I recognize myself less in his books than in those of others or than in the laborious tuning of a guitar. Years ago, I tried ridding myself of him and I went from myths of the outlying slums of the city to games with time and infinity, but those games are now part of Borges, and I will have to turn to other things. And so, my life is a running away, and I lose everything and everything is left to oblivion or to the other man.

Which of us is writing this page I don't know.

What noted writer of recent times has not felt his private life invaded by his life as a celebrity? William Faulkner kept the two parts of his existence in watertight compartments. Samuel Beckett shied away from all publicity. Ernest Hemingway did the opposite and parodied himself to the point where he seemed more and more to be living up to a self he had created in his writings. Borges's case was different. For years, recognition in his own country had consisted of the attention of a small group. By the time his international fame came, he was old. He frequently told an anecdote about the time in the early 1940s when he worked in a municipal library and a fellow worker remarked to him what a strange coincidence it was that there was a writer, mentioned in some handbook or other of Argentine authors, who had the same name and was born in the same year as Borges. The gap between the private and the public Borges was never vast. Hence, perhaps, the more niggling and quarrelsome nature of the conflict.

The third piece is a poem called 'The Watcher', which dates from 1971. It has an obvious resemblance to 'Borges and Myself', but its real interest lies in its striking differences. In 'Borges and Myself', the private and public man are, as the piece tells us, on reasonable terms – though we do feel a certain reluctance on the private man's side. There is a bemused detachment, a resignation, between these two selves. One feeds the other, losing himself in and surrendering himself to the other, but in an uncomplaining way. In the poem, however, there is warring and hatred between the selves. And this time the selves are not divisible into public and private. This time, though there is an 'I' and a 'he', the split is in a single private self. The ironic humour of 'Borges and Myself' turns to bitterness in the poem; the detachment and the clear separateness of the selves in the former are blurred in the latter, where a shift keeps taking place, so that the 'I' is sometimes two and sometimes one.

THE WATCHER

The light comes in and I awake. There he is.

He starts by telling me his name, which is (of course) my own.

I return to the slavery that's lasted more than seven times ten
    years.

He thrusts his memory on me.

He thrusts on me the petty drudgery of each day, the fact of
    dwelling in a body.

I am his old nurse; he makes me wash his feet.

He lies in wait for me in mirrors, in mahogany, in shop-
    windows.

Some woman or other has rejected him and I must share his
    hurt.

He now dictates this poem to me, and I do not like it.

He forces me into the hazy apprenticeship of stubborn Anglo-
    Saxon.

He has converted me to the idolatrous worship of dead sol-
    diers, to whom perhaps I would have nothing to say.

At the last flight of the stairs, I feel him by my side.

He is in my steps, in my voice.

I hate everything about him.

I note with satisfaction that he can barely see.

I'm inside a circular cell and the endless wall is closing in.

Neither of us deceives the other, but both of us are lying.

We know each other too well, inseparable brother.

You drink the water from my cup and eat my bread.

The door of suicide is open, but theologians hold that I'll be there in the far shadow of the other kingdom, waiting for myself.

Speaking about the poem before a group of students, Borges said:

In 'The Watcher' I am interested in the feeling I get every morning when I awake and find that I am Borges. The first thing I do is think of my many worries. Before awakening, I was nobody, or perhaps everybody and everything … but waking up, I feel cramped, and I have to go back to the drudgery of being Borges…. [This] is something deep down within myself – the fact that I feel constrained to be a particular individual, living in a particular city, in a particular time, and so on. This might be thought of as a variation on the Jekyll and Hyde motif. Stevenson thought of the division in ethical terms, but here the division is hardly ethical. It is between the high and fine idea of being all things or nothing in particular, and the fact of being changed into a single man. It is the difference between pantheism – for all we know, we are God when we are asleep – and being merely Mr. Borges….

In the poem, the circular wall is closing in, just as in 'Conjectural Poem' the circle is tightening with the ring of gaucho militia closing in on Laprida, just as in 'In Praise of Darkness' all roads are converging. In each case, the revelation of the true self is imminent. But in 'The Watcher' there is a bleak twist to the idea of the double. Here the confrontation comes after death, and neither revelation nor resolution is hinted at. Presumably the two selves are destined to go on warring in the other kingdom. Finally, in the commentary about 'The Watcher' some new philosophical notions are introduced. Farther along I will discuss these in terms of their mystical implications.

When 'The Watcher' first appeared in a Buenos Aires newspaper, many readers found it a declaration of utter despair. They assumed that Borges had fallen into a deep depression, and they were alarmed by the reference to suicide. I related this to Borges and was assured by him that the poem was only a fiction after all. For my part, I knew that it was and that it wasn't. I knew that Borges's recurring feelings of intense self-disgust were real enough. They are exactly the feelings he attributes to Juan Dahlmann in the hospital in the days following his operation. As for the suicide reference, this I am satisfied was fictional. The very wording, 'the door of suicide', Borges has suggested, he took from Stevenson, who wrote in one of his novels about 'the open door of suicide'. Anyway, joyless and uncomforting as the poem is, I was glad at the time to learn from R.D. Laing, in his book *The Divided Self*, that there is a 'sane schizoid way of being-in-the world'. I believe that this – on one level – is the view of himself that Borges has given us here.

In its original printing, the poem's final line ran, 'in the far shadow of the other kingdom you'll be there waiting for me.' As we were at work on the English translation, Borges had a sudden inspiration, and he asked me what I thought about his changing the line to read, 'I'll be there in the far shadow of the other kingdom, waiting for myself.' I was quick to state my preference. The earlier line seemed to me all too predictable, whereas the new version was more sinister in its implications. What the line now did, I came to realize later, was to emphasize the idea of the fetch. Also, in abandoning the division between the 'I' and 'you' at the end of the poem, the statement of self-loathing, now completely personal, gains in intensity.

But there is another level at work in the poem too, and this one engages Borges in full philosophical play. Let us approach the subject by way of the idea of the Talmudic double, in which a man, in search of God, finds himself. In Shakespeare, Borges saw so many selves that there was no self. 'In him', wrote Borges,

there was no one. Behind his face ... and his words ... there was only a touch of coldness, a dream undreamed by anyone.... By instinct, so as to cover up the fact that he was nobody, he had grown skilled in the trick of making believe he was somebody. There in London he came to the profession to which he was destined – that of the actor, who on a stage plays at being someone else before an audience who plays at taking him for that other person.... No one was ever so many men as this man, who, like the Egyptian Proteus, could run through all of life's guises. Occasionally, he left a confession in some nook of his work, sure it would never be deciphered: Richard II says that in one person he plays many people, and with strange words Iago says, 'I am not what I am.'

This piece, a prose poem two or three pages long, is called – and Borges titled it in English – 'Everything and Nothing'. In the poem 'Emerson' we saw that in not having lived enough the sense of self is unfulfilled. Here, at the other extreme, we have the view that in having lived too much, in having been too many people, the sense of self – one's very identity – is obliterated. This embraces the popular notion (which I regard as extreme and uncommon) of the story-teller's loss of individual identity through his creative involvement in the identity of his fictional characters. The piece closes with this paragraph:

The tale runs that before or after death, when [Shakespeare] stood face to face with God, he said to Him, 'I, who in vain have been so many men, want to be one man – myself.' The voice of the Lord answered him out of the whirlwind, 'I too have no self; I dreamed the world as you dreamed your work, my Shakespeare, and among the shapes of my dream are you, who, like me, are many men and no one.'

Once again we have the theme of the dreamer and the dreamed. But more intriguing here is how Borges – ever prepared to delve into first causes, the cosmological argument, and the ontological argument – takes the splintering of identity right back to the godhead, the 'author' of all things. Borges's loss of identity, still without resolution, is now projected onto the cosmos.

In 'The Watcher', it seems to me, Borges is putting forth two explanations of the division of self. One concerns the ego, or 'I', at perpetual odds with the other Borges, the inescapable author, the 'he', with his decrepit, dying body. This takes place on the everyday, earthly plane. The other division takes place on some disembodied, spiritual level, and it concerns an aspect of Borges's being that is thwarted by imprisonment in a mortal body. The poem, I believe, embraces both these possibilities.

The cue for expanding on the latter view is provided by Borges's comments, quoted above, about 'The Watcher'. The substance of these remarks, postulated by him previously and more formally in a number of essays, are steeped in Hindu and Buddhist beliefs. That we may all be God when we are asleep, for example, is a notion put forward by Shankara, the eighth- or ninth-century founder of classical Hindu thought. 'Shankara teaches', wrote Borges in his 1950 essay 'From Someone to No One', 'that when we are asleep we are the universe, we are God.' Shankara also maintained that the individual self is independent of the physical body and mental or psychic aspects of the human being. Adopting concepts from Buddhism, the Brahman Shankara worked out two levels of truth – the ordinary pragmatic level and the higher level of transcendent truth, in which it is held that the world is not real. The concept of self in 'The Watcher' approaches this view.

Other ideas that run through the informal commentary and formal works like 'The Watcher', 'Borges and Myself', and 'Everything and Nothing' reflect fundamental Indian tenets. These too Borges explored in the trial ground of essays before refining and making them his own in poetry, fiction, and parable. Self-disgust with an ageing and decaying body, touched on in his essay 'The Forms of a Legend', is a theme that goes back at least to Siddhartha, the Buddha, some 500 years BC. Once, during an eight-week trip abroad, Borges astounded me one morning in London when he announced, 'You must despise me.' As he was blind and frail, at the start of each day I cheerfully acted as his valet. The uncharacteristic outpouring was an obvious reference to his decrepit state. It would have comforted me at the time to have known that Borges, who never declared it, incorporated certain features of Indian philosophical idealism into his daily living. He often regarded the unpleasant or distressing events of life as illusory and therefore seldom discussed them.

As a writer, Borges was a magpie. Out of his broad reading – and for our advantage – he was for ever weaving into his work bits and pieces of Eastern and Western culture.* In an appreciation of Valéry, Borges quotes William Hazlitt on Shakespeare to the effect that 'He was nothing in himself.' Years later, in his parable on Shakespeare – which, as we have seen, is as much a piece on the problem of identity and the self – Borges began with that same judgement: 'In him there was no one.' But by then Borges brimmed with Hindu and Buddhist lore, so that now he could also bring to bear on his new ideas all his old irony. In Borges's view, Shakespeare – to hide the fact that he was nobody – made believe he was somebody. But unhappy with his lot after twenty years of writing and producing plays and pretending, Shakespeare quits the theatre, for, at long last, 'He had to be someone....' In retirement, as a 'someone', what does he bequeath the world? Nothing but a 'dry testament'. Not for the Bard, then, the high and fine idea of everything and nothing, the intellectual Hinduism of the union of the individual soul with the whole universe, or the Buddhist super-conscious transcendental state of peace and freedom.

* A few years ago, I wrote in the foreword to a volume of stories from Argentina that 'Argentines have always been notorious magpies, bringing back bits and pieces of foreign culture for their own enrichment and enlightenment.... In our own century, literature knows no greater magpie than Jorge Luis Borges.' It was this magpie trait that made him a darling of the universities, especially those of America. To deal with a difficult-to-classify Borges they even invented a branch of study called Comparative Literature, a term which – owing to the American tendency to be in a hurry – was quickly shortened to Comp Lit.

The bitterness of 'The Watcher' suggests the depth of Borges's struggle to reconcile the drudgery of being Mr Borges with the desire to be everybody and nobody, to balance our more mundane Western way of experiencing life and the physical world with a loss of self and attainment of transcendent truth. Contentedness with the present moment in all its potential fullness is the desired *modus vivendi* of both Eastern and Western mystical traditions. 'It's our duty to be happy,' Borges often told me in difficult times. And in one poem, he wrote,

a man who has learned to express thanks
for the days' modest alms:
sleep, routine, the taste of water ...
may feel suddenly ...
a mysterious happiness ...

In this view, Borges was at the same time at home (and not at home) in two worlds, or two dimensions of reality. One was the cramped, mortal, and conditional physical world that we all know, day in and day out – a world of ignorance, limitation, separateness, and blind groping for an adequate identity and for wholeness. The other was an unconfined, timeless, and unconditional spiritual 'world', of which we are afforded occasional glimpses – a world of perfect knowledge and the loss of separate identity, or ego, or self, in an ineffable greater cosmic Self. At the very least, Borges was both haunted and 'consoled' by the possibility of such a parallel reality.

Borges recognized in himself a tendency 'to judge philosophical or religious ideas for their aesthetic content or even for what in them is odd or extraordinary.' Here lay the basis of his all-pervasive scepticism. (In our daily affairs, I sometimes mistook this for resignation and fatalism.) Doubt and uncertainty informed much of his view of the world and lent colour to so many of his witticisms. Take this one: 'The longer you put off publishing, the better. And if you put it off altogether, perhaps that is best of all.' For a writer, what more telling remark on the obliteration of self?

And yet, and yet – to deny the succession of time, to deny the self, to deny the universe, are measures of outward despair and inner consolation. Our lot … is not terrible because it is unreal; it is terrible because it is irreversible and ironbound. Time is the substance of which I am made. Time is a river that bears me along, but I am the river; it is a tiger that ravages me, but I am the tiger; it is a fire that consumes me, but I am the fire. The world, alas, is real; I, alas, am Borges.

Despite its echoes of pantheism and the Bhagavad Gita and Whitman, the essential scepticism of this statement is perfect Borges. The assertion is also a measure of how profoundly felt was his sense of simultaneous existence in two apparently contradictory realms of reality. In the end, closing the circle of his inquiry and exploration, I believe that these words were his last word and that in them Borges touched his own concept of eternity.

Evaristo Carriego: Borges as Biographer

Occasionally, he left a confession in some nook of his work,
sure it would never be deciphered....

'Everything and Nothing'

I

Evaristo Carriego, a biographical study conceived
and written in the late 1920s and first published in
1930, is the earliest volume of Jorge Luis Borges's
prose that we have in English and, until recently,
the earliest that he still allowed to remain in print in
Spanish. But who was Evaristo Carriego? He was a
minor Argentine poet who died in 1912 at the age of
twenty-nine, the man who, in Borges's words, 'discovered the literary possibilities of the ragged and
run-down outskirts of [Buenos Aires] – the Palermo
of my boyhood.' *Evaristo Carriego*, in fact, is not
very much about Evaristo Carriego (1883–1912);
it is really about Borges himself and about old-time
Buenos Aires. As such, it illuminates certain stretches
of Borges's subsequent writing and provides startling

insights into his later attitudes and ironic statements about the prose – suppressed for so long – that preceded *Evaristo Carriego*. The book is useful to any reader who, already familiar with the major stories and essays, wants a glimpse into another corner of the still incomplete but masterly canvas of Borges's whole work.

II

When *Evaristo Carriego* appeared, it was Borges's seventh published book. Three poetry collections (gathering eighty-four poems) and three volumes of essays (gathering sixty-eight pieces) had come before – all in a truly prolific seven-year span that is still more remarkable when we consider that numerous other pieces contributed to magazines and newspapers of the time were, until only two years ago, left uncollected. In his 1970 memoir, the 'Autobiographical Essay' written for *The Aleph and Other Stories*, Borges dismissed the three prose volumes as 'reckless compilations' and went on to say that

In 1929, that third book of essays won the Second Municipal Prize of three thousand pesos, which in those days was a lordly sum of money. I was, for one thing, to acquire with it a secondhand set of the Eleventh Edition of the *Encyclopædia Britannica*. For another, I was assured a year's leisure and decided I would write a longish book on a wholly Argentine subject. My mother wanted me to write about any of three really worthwhile poets – Ascasubi, Almafuerte, or Lugones. I now wish I had. Instead, I chose to write about a nearly invisible popular poet, Evaristo Carriego.

How much of this statement is true? How much a deliberate false track – and if so, why? A 1978 biography of Borges, relying on memoir here rather than on first-hand investigation, leads to some flimsy judgements. In 'choosing Carriego as a fit subject for a major work,' the biographer wrote, Borges 'was quietly stressing his rebellion against family values,' thereby indicating 'a decision to challenge established literary values.' Nonsense. Borges was simply being himself and following his own bent. The hard facts, I will show, reward us with different and far richer conclusions.

Evaristo Carriego has two sets of roots – one, in articles and poems written by Borges long before he began work on the eventual book; the other, in Borges family history. The volume that gained that 1929 prize was the formerly suppressed *El idioma de los argentinos*, originally published the previous year. On the reverse of the title page, in a list of other books by Borges, the last entry reads – and I translate – 'In progress: *A Life of Evaristo Carriego*.' Clearly, then, *Evaristo Carriego* was not the result of a last-minute decision foisted on Borges by the advent of an unexpected gift.

In an essay dated January 1926, 'The Extent of My Hope' – the title piece from the second of the once suppressed collections of this period – Borges informs us in a flush of nationalistic fervour that a list of the truly Argentine writers of the first quarter of this century 'must include the names of Evaristo Carriego, Macedonio Fernández, and Ricardo Güiraldes.' As if in pursuit of this notion, the same collection contains the piece 'Carriego y el sentido del arrabal' (Carriego and His Awareness of the City's Outskirts), whose half-dozen pages amount to no less than a trial balloon, a rehearsal, for the book-length essay of 1930. Both the shape and essence of the later study are here in embryo: an opening description of Palermo, a swipe at José Gabriel's 1921 biography of Carriego, the gist of the critical judgements. Whole passages are even lifted from the 1926 essay and used almost verbatim in the 1930 book. 'Carriego y el sentido del arrabal' begins by affirming that Carriego's poems 'are the soul of the Argentine soul' and ends by announcing that 'This all-too-brief discourse on Carriego has another side, and I must return to the subject one day simply to praise him.'

We can trace these written roots back farther still. In 1925, in the foreword to his second poetry collection, *Luna de enfrente*, Borges wrote that in two pieces 'figures the name of Evaristo Carriego, always as something of a minor deity of Palermo, for that is how I feel about him.' The latter of these two poems, 'Versos de catorce' (Fourteeners), titled after its fourteen-syllable lines, tells us that 'I felt that Palermo's straight streets … spoke to me of Carriego….' The reference to Carriego in the other poem, 'A la calle Serrano', is slight, but because the link with him here lies in the whole piece it is more significant. As these lines were never reprinted in his lifetime after their appearance in the 300-copy first edition of *Luna de enfrente*, they are little known.* Calle Serrano is the name of the street in Palermo on which the Borges family had once lived. 'Calle Serrano,' the poem begins, 'you are no longer the same as at the time of the Centenary' – that is to say, no longer as it was fifteen years earlier, in 1910, when Borges had lived there as a boy and Evaristo Carriego 'never missed a Sunday at our house on his return from the race-track.' In the poems left by Carriego after his death is one called 'El camino de nuestra casa', which loosely translates as 'On Our Street', the exact sense of Borges's title. The subject and the elegiac tone of the two pieces are identical. 'You are as familiar to us as a thing that once was ours and ours alone,' runs Carriego's poem in the rather lovely lines that Borges later singled out in his biography. The holograph facsimile reproduced in the first edition of *Evaristo Carriego*, it should be noted, is from this particular poem.

The second set of roots of Borges's book on Carriego is embedded in Borges family history. Carriego, as well as having been a neighbour, had been a friend

---

* I am not unaware that they were included in a 1926 anthology of vanguard verse.

of Borges's father. As a boy, Borges had listened to the poet recite from memory the 150-odd stanzas of Almafuerte's *Misionero*. Carriego had written prophetically, in verse, of the ten-year-old Borges in his mother's album; an inscribed copy of Carriego's poems had accompanied the Borges clan to Europe in 1914; and Borges, as he tells us in his 'Autobiographical Essay', read and reread them in Geneva.

There is abundant evidence, then, that Borges had been under the spell of Carriego for years. When Borges began the Carriego book he was very nearly Carriego's age at the time of his death. Each had been over the same ground with a first book of verse about Buenos Aires – not the centre of the city but its shabby outlying areas, principally the Palermo where each had lived. Borges's identification with Carriego was close, and the act of writing a book about him was an acknowledgement of this connection. 'Truly I loved the man, on this side idolatry, as much as any.' That is Ben Jonson on Shakespeare, borrowed and condensed by Jorge Luis Borges to appear – in English – as the last sentence and paragraph of Borges's 1930 book on Carriego. Nowhere else in the works of the reticent, reserved Borges – not even in his love poems – are such strong sentiments to be found.* Borges did not write *Evaristo Carriego* by

* Except, of course, in his 'Autobiographical Essay', in which Borges used these same words by Ben Jonson to sum up his feelings about Macedonio Fernández.

chance or whim, nor as an act of rebellion; he wrote the book out of inner necessity.

III

Evaristo Carriego was also written with compelling honesty, which is why it cannot be lightly dismissed as a failure – as it has been – on the grounds that it is neither good biography nor good criticism. In common with all Borges's work, *Evaristo Carriego* is highly personal and even idiosyncratic. As such, it must be judged on its own clearly stated terms. It is not and never set out to be a conventional biography.

In the 1926 'trial' essay, Borges takes a polemical stance when he claims that 'in José Gabriel's mythifying there is a pusillanimous and almost effeminate Carriego who is certainly not the man with the stinging tongue and the endless talker that I knew in my boyhood....' This position is taken up again, obliquely and subtly, in the 1930 essay, in whose second chapter we read:

The events of [Carriego's] life, while infinite and incalculable, are outwardly easy to record, and in his book of 1921 Gabriel has helpfully listed them. Here we learn that Evaristo Carriego was born on 7 May 1883, that he completed three years of high school, that he worked on the editorial staff of *La Protesta*, that he died on 13 October 1912, and other detailed and unvisual information with which the author's disjointed work – which should be to make such information visual – liberally burdens the reader. I believe that a chronological account is inappropriate to Carriego, a man whose life was made up of walks and conversations. To reduce him to a list, to trace the order of his days, seems to me impossible; far better seek his eternity, his patterns. Only a timeless description ... can bring him back to us.

In 1970, over forty years after these words were written, I was to learn how strongly Borges felt that a chronological account of his own life, one also made up of walks and conversations, was inappropriate or at least unsatisfying to him. Despite the acclaim that poured in from all sides following the publication of his 'Autobiographical Essay' (called 'Autobiographical Notes') as a *New Yorker* Profile, Borges baulked at the last moment and would not allow the piece to be translated into Spanish and published in *La Nación*, although we had already arranged for its appearance there. Privately he confessed to me his misgivings about the essay, complaining that there were too many dates in it. The structuring of the piece, its straightforward chronological form, and the researching of dates had been part of my special contribution to the writing of the work. Borges's 1978 biographer, who thought highly enough of the essay to quote it whole and make his book a gloss on it, remarked that it was composed for an Argentine audience. On the contrary, it was conceived and written with the

English-speaking reader in mind. I had wanted it to serve as a kind of introduction to Borges, in his own inimitable words, that would also serve as a frame for his writing at a time when more and more of it was being published in the United States and England. To achieve these ends, I felt – and still feel – that the essay had to be rooted in, and not outside, time. As much as Borges's reaction seemed the result of a sudden whim, it did have a sound philosophical basis in Berkeleyan idealism. At the heart of his famous essay on the denial of time, Borges wrote that 'the chronological pinpointing of an event, of any event under the sun, is not part and parcel of the event.'

It would have been pointless for Borges in 1930 to have gone over the same ground as Gabriel in 1921. To be of value, another book on Carriego had to be different from, even a reaction *against*, the previous one. If José Gabriel's biography could have all of the facts and none of the essence of Carriego, Borges would deliberately set out to write a study that, near enough, contained none of the facts and all of the essence. That second chapter, from which I quoted above, an account of Carriego's life, provides us – if I have managed to count correctly – with six dates. (For a minor bibliographical reason, in my English version of the book, I myself introduced a seventh date.) Two tell us the years certain books appeared (they are not important); two, the years certain events took place (one of them is quite incidental);

and two – the years Carriego was born and died – were, as we have just seen, supplied by Gabriel. We have a man's whole life, then, with but a single vital date furnished us by his biographer. While this may appear nothing short of outrageous, I find it intriguing in its metaphysical implications, which, succinctly, are that

These patterns in Carriego's life that I have described will, I know, bring him closer to us. They repeat him over and over in us, as if Carriego went on living in our lives, as if for a few seconds each one of us were Carriego. I believe that this is literally the case, and that these fleeting moments of becoming him (not of mirroring him), which annihilate the supposed flow of time, are proof of eternity.

Does the book light up the eternity of Carriego? That becomes less a question of the details of the physical life than a critical examination of the creative life. In this respect, Borges's judgements are basically sound, and they are also quite simple: Carriego wrote a handful of good poems, which are not the sentimental ones that have secured his popular fame. What is faulty in the criticism – in the book's third chapter at least – is the perfunctory and limited nature of much of the analysis. Having chosen to discuss a certain set of poems, Borges soon falls into ticking off a list, of dealing with the pieces by rote. But once he abandons this rigid scheme and ranges more widely and deeply – as he does in Chapter IV – his comment comes alive again and we are amply rewarded. In the 'Autobiographical Essay', Borges admits that 'The more I wrote the less I cared about my hero' and also that 'I became more and more interested in old-time Buenos Aires.' If we emend 'my hero' to read 'my hero's poems', there is an element of truth in it. From internal evidence I suspect that the strong opening chapter, on Palermo, was written last, after the biographical and critical sections had begun to pall and still had not yielded up pages enough to fill out a whole volume.

At any rate, the remark about his hero's fate gives a nice insight into why Borges never wrote a novel and a truer reason than his frequently repeated, self-deprecating claim of sheer laziness. Among other things, Borges was simply never able to sustain interest in a single person or set of persons for the span of time and space a novel requires. One has only to examine the pieces in *A Universal History of Infamy* to see this, or his perfect outline for a novel, the seven-page story called 'The Dead Man'. Any man's life, Borges holds in another story, 'is made up essentially *of a single moment* – the moment in which [he] finds out, once and for all, who he is.' That, of course, is the moment of his eternity; all the rest is mere data, or, put another way, as Borges neatly does at the outset of *Evaristo Carriego*, 'reality comes to us ... not in the proliferation of facts but in the enduring nature of particular elements.'

The difference between his book's projected title in 1928 and its final title in 1930 is telling. *Evaristo Carriego* should be taken neither as biography nor as literary criticism but as an exercise in belles-lettres.

IV

It is unfortunate that by shrouding his study of Carriego in mystery and belittling it Borges has paved the way for critics to misunderstand it. 'Some books are to be tasted,' wrote Bacon, 'others to be swallowed, and some few to be chewed and digested.' If the student of Borges chews this work, if he or she reads it with diligence and attention, considerable pleasure and profit can be found in its pages.

In *Evaristo Carriego* we find a very early use of the technique of random enumeration learned from Whitman, exercised throughout the Borges canon, and brought to perfection in a certain page of his story 'The Aleph'. We find the first reference to his interest in the techniques of film-making, a last ultraist image (ultraism was a form of imagism championed by Borges for several years in the early 1920s and later repudiated), the inadvertent title of a tale unwritten for another four years, the growing command of his bookishness, so that – in the span of a single paragraph – he can smoothly clarify a point with quotations from or references to

Shaw, the Gnostics, Blake, Hernández, Almafuerte, and Quevedo. On one page, speaking of Carriego's fondness for tales of blood and thunder, Borges recounts an episode concerning the death of the outlaw Juan Moreira, 'who went from the ardent games of the brothel to the bullets and bayonets of the police.' Immediately we recognize here the germ of the story 'The Night of the Gifts', which Borges did not commit to paper for forty-five or so more years. On another page we read that Carriego 'never exhausted the night', and here we spot one of Borges's favourite (and sometimes abused) rhetorical devices – the hypallage, the figure of speech that reverses the order of a customary proposition, or, as Borges himself once put it, the figure in which an epithet is defined by what surrounds it (Milton's studious lamps, Lugones's arid camel). Somewhere else, in reading how, as a boy, Carriego presented himself to the local political boss of Palermo – he 'told Paredes he was Evaristo Carriego, from Honduras Street' – we can hear the way, in a later sketch by Borges, one Bill Harrigan introduces himself after he has gunned down his first Mexican: 'Well, I'm Billy the Kid, from New York.' Or, in coming upon the words 'penetrating revolvers', we recognize another hypallage, one that Borges was to repeat almost exactly in another part of *A Universal History of Infamy* three or four years later. Or we stumble on an unusual and uncharacteristic blind spot, such as the notion that Kipling was of mixed English and Indian blood. I am puzzled why Borges never corrected this in the book's second edition twenty-five years later, when he set one or two other matters straight. In 1937 he reviewed Kipling's autobiography, which surely made him see the error. It is in the Carriego book too that Borges for the first time borrowed, or recycled, bits of his earlier work, a habit he was later to make himself famous for. (In this case, an article on the popular Argentine card-game *truco*, which had already appeared in *El idioma de los argentinos*, and – as mentioned earlier – passages from an essay on Carriego printed in *El tamaño de mi esperanza*.)

Evaristo Carriego also affords us an opportunity to delve into that aspect of Borges's prose of the 1920s of which he has remarked, 'I was doing my best to write Latin in Spanish....' If a heavy reliance on Latin syntax is a mark of certain of his early prose, then the book on Carriego clearly falls into the category of early prose. A look into this Latinate Spanish will serve to illustrate one of the difficulties of translating various passages of Borges's work at the same time as it helps account for the uneven quality of many of his translations into English.

Take an example from Chapter II. Here Borges lists a few of the elements that made up the pattern of Carriego's daily life. The first of these is '*los desabridos despertares caseros*' – literally, 'the insipid waking ups domestic'. There are no case endings to guide us; we have only the required grammatical agreement of the two adjectives with the noun. Since 'waking up' is in the plural, it obviously means waking up more than once, or waking up every morning. But '*caseros*' is trying to function as an ablative, the case used to express the relation of separation. So this becomes 'at home'. Roughly, then, we have 'the insipid waking-up-every-morning at home'. When we wake up and where overlap enough to make one of them unnecessary. Dealing next with the first adjective, '*desabridos*', and amplifying a bit to express the plural of 'waking up', we refine further and come up with 'the humdrum business of waking up in the morning'. Now, while I may have achieved accuracy here – that is, got the meaning – there are any number of ways of saying the same thing: 'the pointlessness of getting up in the morning', 'the daily drudgery of getting out of bed', or, as I finally opted, 'the unpleasant business of getting up in the morning'. Accuracy alone does not make a translation good, but it is the starting point of good translation. The problems presented by Latin constructions in Borges's writing baffle native Argentine readers as much as they do Borges's translators, nor are academic credentials a guarantee of unravelling or understanding exactly all that Borges writes. A knowledge of Spanish, too, is often only a starting point.

V

Evaristo Carriego has had two lives. There was the modest first edition of 118 text pages, divided into five chapters, with two appendices that were later elevated to chapter status, and the whole bound in pink wrappers. A quarter of a century later, in 1955, came a new edition, filled out with a half-dozen miscellaneous pieces written in the early 1950s (chapters VIII through XII). For the most part, these round out the book in terms of old-time Buenos Aires and not of Carriego. As the work of Borges's rich maturity, they stand in little need of elucidation.

Two of the additions, however, are corrective, and as such they shed light on the key problem of why Borges found it necessary to suppress so much of his early writing. The brief 1950 foreword to an edition of Carriego's poems contradicts nothing Borges wrote about Carriego in 1930; but neither does the piece say anything about the poetry. Three pages long and set out with tremendous reserve, the perspective is one of great distance. Obviously, Borges was refraining from a blatant condemnation of the poems; one cannot very well damn the volume one has agreed to preface. The piece's brilliance is in its speculation about how Carriego became Carriego, but that brilliance resides in a display of Borges's imaginative powers and may, really, have little to do with the factual truth about Carriego.

By what they do not tell us, by what they hold back, these pages mark the end of Borges's enthralment to Carriego.

The long essay on the tango's history is another matter. A complete rewriting of a piece published early in 1927 and later collected in *El idioma de los argentinos*, its viewpoint and its conclusions are an about-face. The first essay is nationalistic to the point of xenophobia, while the later work is not only universal but also berates much of the narrowmindedness of the earlier judgements. Comparison of these two pieces reveals the extent of Borges's journey through the years from callowness to maturity.

Publicly and privately, Borges stated that he kept his early work out of print because it was either badly written or of little value. While indeed some of it is ephemeral and some less strikingly composed, he himself gave the lie to this claim and at the same time paid tribute to the worth of certain of the writing in question by recasting or otherwise re-using it. What Borges was really trying to suppress was content as much as form; I refer to a display of vehement nativist sentiment, a point of view that a few years later came to haunt and embarrass him. Unable to abolish these outpourings, he could only live them down – beyond rewriting and cleansing a few – by keeping the entire lot out of print. This, of course, was greatly to his credit although somewhat to our loss, for, in sticking to his decision, Borges had been forced to throw out some good things along with the bad.

Several years after his death, in 1986, Borges's estate licensed the reissue of his first three volumes of essays. *El tamaño de mi esperanza* (1926) appeared in 1993; and *Inquisiciones* (1925) and *El idioma de los argentinos* (1928), in 1994. Additionally, a 462-page volume of (mainly) hitherto uncollected early writings, *Textos recobrados 1919–1929*, was published in 1997. Further volumes of uncollected work are apparently contemplated.

This phenomenon is interesting in light of the remarks Borges made about his early prose in his 1970 autobiography. There, in repudiating these collections, he claimed that 'Until a few years ago, if the price were not too stiff, I would buy up copies and burn them.' I had heard him say this in public a number of times but to me it was a pretty tale whose truth I held in doubt. When we were writing the story of his life, he was irked when I asked him to speak of these books. Borges wanted to pass over them in silence. We argued the point and reached a compromise. He was to write:

... I feel only the remotest kinship with the work of these years. Three of the four essay collections – whose names are best forgotten – I have never allowed to be reprinted. In fact, when in 1953 my present publisher ... proposed to bring out my 'complete writings,' the only reason I accepted was that it would allow me to keep these preposterous volumes suppressed.

He then went on for a page and a half to catalogue in detail the stylistic sins of the bulk of these early essays. 'These sins', he concluded,

were fine writing, local color, a quest for the unexpected, and a seventeenth-century style. Today I no longer feel guilty over these excesses; those books were written by somebody else.

Indeed they were. With snipes at Sarmiento, Argentina's great champion of civilized values, with an occasional anti-European and anti-North American slant, they were certainly not the work of the Borges we admire today for his uncompromising universality. Nor were they the work of the Borges who in the 1940s was made to taste vulgar nativism in its crude Peronist form when, because he had sided with the Allies during the war, he was 'promoted' out of his library job 'to the inspectorship of poultry and rabbits in the public markets'.

As for Carriego, did Borges disown him, too, along with the unacceptable nationalism because, on looking back, the two seemed part and parcel of each other? I believe he did. But I believe that Carriego was also disowned in a less than generous bid by Borges to cover his own tracks. In a story, he once wrote – paraphrasing Dr Johnson – that 'nobody ...

likes owing anything to his contemporaries.' In addition to Carriego, Borges in later years retreated on writers like Macedonio Fernández, Ricardo Güiraldes, and Miguel de Unamuno, all of whom, once highly proclaimed by him, he ultimately dropped from his pantheon. In the time I spent with Borges I witnessed the process unfold and accelerate in proportion to the spread of his international fame. When I recognized what he was doing, I even penned myself a note to the effect that the influence – the uncomfortable influence – of Macedonio, Güiraldes, Unamuno, and Carriego on Borges merited serious study.

In Carriego's case there was more than the mark he left on a number of Borges's early poems. Such laconic lines as these, about fading daguerreotypes, from 'Empty Drawing Room':

Amid the brocade's dimness
the mahogany suite continues
its everlasting conversation.
... the light
slices through the windowpanes
and humbles the senile armchairs
and corners and strangles
the shriveled voice
of these ancestors.

or these, from 'Plainness':

The garden's grillwork gate
opens with the ease of a page
in a much-thumbed book ...

or these, from 'The Recoleta':

We mistake this peace for death,
believing we yearn for our end
when we yearn for sleep and oblivion.

have their roots in the homely verses of Carriego's
best work. In a 1926 article about Buenos Aires in
poetry, Borges singled out four Carriego poems – 'El
alma del suburbio', 'En el barrio', 'El guapo', and
'El amasijo' – for the way they said everything about
the neighbourhood of Palermo as well as for their
perfection. Certain elements in these poems do not
stand up to analysis. In one – for example – dark, deserted streets give back both the footsteps of passers-
by and the cries of the old-fashioned policeman
on his beat. Too much traffic, in my view, for sup-
posedly empty night-time streets. But the imagery is
uncluttered and succinct, and the music of the lines
is understated and flawless:

Devuelven las oscuras calles desiertas
el taconeo tardo de los paseantes ...

Similarly, we read in another:

Ya los de la casa se van acercando
al rincón del patio que adorna la parra,
y el cantor del barrio se sienta, templando,
con mano nerviosa la dulce guitarra.

But Carriego left something more indelible in Borges than the traces we find here in the poems. The real spell cast by the poet of Palermo over Borges concerns a large chunk of Borges's subject matter. I refer to his fascination with knives, knife fighters, and local toughs, which became the theme of so many of his stories and poems. It was a spell that Borges never woke from, an obsession that he never outgrew and that even loomed larger as he grew older.

Much of this world is contained in a single Carriego poem, 'El guapo' – 'The Tough'. The neighbourhood admires him, the first stanza opens. Admiring courage himself, he won renown for his daring. The verses speak of his triumphs and glory. Deep scars, violent stigmata, criss-cross his face, and these ineradicable bloody adornments, caprices of the knife, flatter him. The names of illustrious knife fighters of the past, Juan Moreira and Santos Vega, are evoked. With his guitar and his hat cocked over his eyes, the tough is both poet and outlaw.

It was out of material of this sort that Borges created what he termed his 'myths of the outlying slums of the city'. The tone and flavour of those myths were Carriego's, and the very vocabulary of this little domain – which Borges ultimately appropriated for himself – is all here in Carriego's verse narratives. Borges's best writing about knife fighting and fighters is contained in a 1952 piece, 'The Challenge', one of those incomparable gems of his that is part narrative, part essay. In 1955, he retitled the piece and, unfortunately, buried it in the middle of a longish essay on the tango for the new edition of his book on Carriego. There, appearing as a sub-chapter, it has been overlooked ever since. The change in title is significant. Now he called it 'The Cult of Courage'. '*Cultor del coraje*' – that is, cultivator, or admirer, of courage – is what Carriego terms his tough in the first line of 'El guapo'.

In one of Borges's late stories, 'Rosendo's Tale', there is mention of a 'letter written by some kid all dressed in black, who ... made up poems about tenements and filth – stuff that no refined public would dream of reading.' The reference to the 'kid' is, of course, an oblique, affectionate tip of the hat to Carriego. The remark about 'filth' is a bit of a private joke and self-mockery. Borges's aged mother, doña Leonor, had always been appalled that her son should choose to write about such riff-raff.

In the Carriego sonnet 'Como en los buenos tiempos', remarkably, I find a prime source for 'The Aleph', a story Borges wrote in 1945. In the tale, the narrator renders homage to the memory of his once beloved and now dead Beatriz Viterbo by paying a sentimental visit each year – on her birthday – to her family home, where photographs of her in various settings and poses still adorn the cluttered drawing-room. The narrator of Carriego's poem, too, addresses his beloved, also deceased, in a similar room. Sometimes, a bit sad, he says, I look at your photograph, full of life, although you have been gone for a long, long time. The portrait tells so little. Losing you perhaps was better than to have loved you and watched your shame of growing old. Still, I would be lying if I were to say I no longer hear you at the piano, which has never been opened again, and feel the emotion of that now distant time when you were kin to the moon. In Borges, of course, there is the ironic edge we expect of him, but otherwise the evocations in the story and poem are identical.

Borges was the biographer of the eternal moment, and the Aleph he invented – that 'single gigantic instant' containing 'infinite things' – is perhaps its symbol. His own eternal moment, as he told us in so many nooks of his work, was the period of his boyhood in Palermo, when he 'grew up in a garden, behind a fence of iron palings, and in a library of endless English books.' It was to that world, time and time again in his imagination, that he returned.

Borges and His Sources:
A Universal History of Infamy

Speaking nearly half a century later of his first collection of poems, *Fervor de Buenos Aires* (1923), Borges said, 'looking back on it now, I think I have never strayed beyond that book. I feel that all my subsequent [verse] has only developed themes first taken up there; I feel that all during my lifetime I have been rewriting that one book.'

A case may be made, it seems to me, for claiming the same of his first collection of essays, *Inquisiciones* (1925); all his subsequent essays have only developed themes first taken up there. Again, the same may be said of his earliest work of prose fiction, *A Universal History of Infamy* (1935). All Borges's subsequent short stories have only developed themes – and techniques – initially taken up in that book. It is this third proposition that interests me here.

A Universal History of Infamy was Borges's ninth full-length book and his sixth of prose. More significantly, *Historia universal de la infamia* – to give it its original title – is the first of Borges's five full volumes of narrative fiction. The story collections that followed it were *The Garden of Branching Paths*

(1942; enlarged and reissued as *Ficciones*, in 1944, and again enlarged under the latter title in 1956), *The Aleph* (1949; enlarged in 1952), *Doctor Brodie's Report* (1970), and *The Book of Sand* (1975). There were four additional stories at the time of Borges's death, in 1986. It should be stressed that the number of these volumes was only five. (He once remarked to me that he had the smallest bag of tricks of any writer going.) If we stop to consider, then, that Borges's world-wide fame derives from a body of work this small – in all he published little more than fifty short stories – it seems only right to regard any one of these sets of tales as important.

Or so one would have judged. The American poet Richard Howard has said of *A Universal History of Infamy* that it is

One of the most brilliant, disturbing and preposterous of all Borges' books. Written in the style of incredulity, it jeopardizes all styles, even its own, and reminds us, once again, that we share our century with the greatest confidence man in literature.

The deeper implications of the book's language and stylistic devices were masterfully treated in an essay by David Gallagher, a former Oxford don, who pointed out that in its aestheticism, in its 'conspicuous language, its fine, lapidary arrangements of words', *A Universal History of Infamy* eloquently [expressed] the contention that reality and its interpretation are affairs of the mind, that therefore there are as many realities as there are minds or interpretations, and that where several evaluations of a given event are possible, none can be said to be defective.

Not surprisingly, Emir Rodríguez Monegal, a critic and biographer of Borges, made the claim that *A Universal History of Infamy* was 'the book that literally transformed the Spanish prose of the thirties and whose long echoes can still be heard in [Gabriel García Márquez's] "One Hundred Years of Solitude"....' García Márquez himself has paid tribute to Borges's 'extraordinary capacity for verbal artifice', describing how he reads him every night and on his travels carries around in a suitcase Borges's complete works. The Mexican novelist Carlos Fuentes goes even further, saying that without Borges's prose 'there simply would not be a modern Spanish-American novel' and that Borges 'constitutes a new Latin-American language....'

And yet, for a wide and often absurd variety of reasons, *A Universal History of Infamy* has become a book around which much confusion and speculation have grown up. It is, in fact, the least understood of all Borges's works. I would suggest that one of the chief reasons for this has to do with that most beguilingly subversive hallmark of Borges's style – his seriously playful misappropriation of scholarly sources.

Consider, for example, the nature of the book itself. What exactly is it – fiction or fact? Its first section, called 'A Universal History of Infamy', is made up – apparently – of brief biographies (none exceeds ten pages) of a gallery of seven rogues and scoundrels, male and female, drawn from several lands and from various periods in time. Such reckless brevity, so blatant a want of comprehensiveness, can only make of the slim volume a mockery both of universality and history. In like manner, the very grandiloquence of the title can only be tongue-in-cheek. Borges's own remarks about the book seem less helpful than confusing. In a preface to the original edition, we are told that its contents are 'exercises in narrative prose' and that they stem from 'rereadings of Stevenson and Chesterton, and also from Sternberg's early films....' Appended to the volume, we find a 'List of Sources' that gives exact bibliographical information about the works on which the little biographies seem to be based. Of the ten titles in this list, one is in German, all the others are in English, and they range from Mark Twain and a volume of the *Encyclopædia Britannica* (Eleventh Edition) to a history of Persia, a history of piracy, and *The Saga of Billy the Kid*. On the face of it, this seems a plausible enough catalogue of books, even if characterized by somewhat out-of-the-way reading. But, of course, if we know anything at all about Borges we know him to have been a master of just such reading habits.

The book's next section is made up of a full-length short story called 'Streetcorner Man'. Another preface, written in 1954 for the second edition, informs us that this is a straightforward story, and of it Borges tells that he first 'signed it with the name of one of his great grandfathers, Francisco Bustos', and that the tale 'has enjoyed an unusual and somewhat mystifying success.' Then there is the book's third and final section, called 'Etcetera'. This seems the oddest part of all. It contains eight pieces, some of them so brief as to be hardly more than snippets. One of the prefaces tells us, 'As for the examples of magic that close the volume, I have no other rights to them than those of translator and reader.' And, fittingly enough, sources are provided at the close of each piece – title and author. Two come from The Thousand and One Nights (even the particular number of each night is meticulously supplied), a third is from a little-known account of exploration in central Africa by Sir Richard Burton, two others are from works by Emanuel Swedenborg, one is from a fourteenth-century Spanish classic, and the last two are from totally obscure works and completely unknown authors – H. Gering's *Anhang zur Heimskringla* and J.A. Suárez Miranda's *Travels of Praiseworthy Men*.

Perhaps the most flustering thing of all about *A Universal History of Infamy* is its author's two forewords. Both belittle and minimize the book. The earlier one states that the collection's exercises 'overly exploit certain tricks.' Then come bewildering statements to the effect that reading is somehow superior to writing. 'Sometimes I suspect that good readers are even blacker and rarer swans than good writers,' says Borges. And, 'Reading is an activity which comes after that of writing; it is more modest, more unobtrusive, more intellectual.' The second foreword, written nearly twenty years later, is even more severe. It tells us that 'The very title of these pages flaunts their baroque character', having previously defined the baroque as a style that 'only too obviously exhibits or overdoes its own tricks.' This time the work is defined as 'ambiguous exercises', and the foreword goes on to say of them that

They are the irresponsible game of a shy young man who dared not write stories and so amused himself by falsifying and distorting (without any aesthetic justification whatever) the tales of others.

Harsher still is this judgement:

The theologians of the Great Vehicle point out that the essence of the universe is emptiness. Insofar as they refer to that particle of the universe which is this book, they are entirely right. Scaffolds and pirates populate it, and the word 'infamy' in the title is thunderous, but behind the sound and fury there is nothing. The book is no more than appearance, than a surface of images....

A second reason for the wealth of misunderstanding about *A Universal History of Infamy* has to do with Borges's private and sometimes reckless opinions of the book. These were often even more disparaging than the statements made in his forewords. He once told me that the book was badly written to the point of embarrassment, which is simply untrue, and that he was sometimes sorry he had allowed it to be re-issued. Not infrequently these remarks found their way into print. Back in 1967, for example, when Borges first went to Harvard, he told an interviewer, Richard Burgin, that

all the stories in that book were kind of jokes or fakes. But now I don't think very much of that book, it amused me when I wrote it, but I can hardly recall who the characters were.

Six years later, when *A Universal History of Infamy* was first published in Britain, a reviewer, quoting these words and linking them with others about the book's being 'the irresponsible game of a shy young man', etc., concluded − one should say was led to conclude − 'I believe we must take [Borges] at his word.' Even considering his headlong tendency to 'disown his own past', I wonder whether Borges would have expressed himself so carelessly to Burgin had he known that their taped conversations would be made into a book and that the book might be used in this way to damn valuable work. I suspect not. When in 1970 Borges and I were writing his autobiography, we found ways of being both serious and informative about *A Universal History of Infamy* while still preserving some of Borges's reservations about a book he had written half a lifetime earlier. So prevalent were his self-deprecating and self-damaging pronouncements elsewhere, however, that I was to read in the *New York Times Book Review* (7 May 1972) of Borges's well-known 'reluctance to authorize a translation of "Historia Universal de la Infamia"....' By that date, my English version of the book was not only finished but also in production. The translation was even one in which Borges himself had taken a large hand.

A third reason for the general lack of serious attention that *A Universal History of Infamy* has commanded is that, although the earliest of Borges's fiction to be written, it was among the last to have been translated into English. Coming to us long after the brilliant and now-famous stories of *Ficciones* and *The Aleph*, *A Universal History of Infamy* – a book by nature ambiguous, a book disparaged by Borges himself – has had about it all the air of an anticlimax. That this should no longer be true I hope to prove in these pages.

My discoveries stem from my translation of the book at the author's side in Buenos Aires. When at the end of his stay at Harvard Borges invited me to join him in Argentina, I began to investigate what work we might do together there. It was at this time that I first spoke to him about making an English version of *A Universal History of Infamy*. I had found the book entertaining and I also knew that it was thriving in Spanish, French, German, and Italian editions. With the rapidly growing interest in Borges at the time, an English translation of the book seemed inevitable. But Borges's reaction to my proposal was unprecedented. Usually even-tempered and easy-going, he was now as close to violence and abuse as I ever saw him. It was at this point that he said that the book was badly written and that he confessed his unhappiness about having allowed it back into print. Not only did I meet with a flat refusal, but he also hinted he would have no more to do with me if I breathed another word about the subject. I shut up. What else could I do?

A few days later, the late John Murchison, the Harvard graduate student who was Borges's secretary that year, told me that Borges, still fuming, had asked him what he thought of my madness. Quite matter-of-factly, Murchison replied that he considered the book charming, and he saw no reason why it should not be translated. Shortly after, Borges repeated all this to me in an amused, offhand way, as if to suggest that Murchison too was mad. On this occasion, however, since it was Borges who had broached the subject, I felt free to speak up. I pointed out that since the translation rights to his work were administered by his publisher, anyone who wrote to them to buy those rights could do so without Borges's even knowing about it. If he and I didn't make the translation together, I said, someone else might come along and perhaps not do it as well. At least we could curb the book's defects, I added. That convinced him. 'In that case,' Borges said, 'we won't just translate it, we'll rewrite it.' But it was not until four years and four books later that the project would be started. We found out then what I had known all along – that the drastic measure of rewriting the book was unnecessary.

Let us turn to the story called 'The Disinterested Killer Bill Harrigan' and, taking it chapter by chapter, look into its stylistic and historical sources. In this way, we may discover what is fact and what is fiction. The piece begins with the following introduction:

An image of the desert wilds of Arizona, first and foremost, an image of the desert wilds of Arizona and New Mexico – a country famous for its silver and gold camps, a country of breathtaking open spaces, a country of monumental mesas and soft colors, a country of bleached skeletons picked clean by buzzards. Over this whole country, another image – that of Billy the Kid, the hard rider firm on his horse, the young man with the relentless six-shooters, sending out invisible bullets which (like magic) kill at a distance.

The desert veined with precious metals, arid and blinding-bright. The near child who on dying at the age of twenty-one owed to the justice of grown men twenty-one deaths – 'not counting Mexicans.'

The scene is set and the hero presented. The treatment is cinematic; we can almost feel the panning camera, then the close-ups. It is clear both here and throughout the story that Borges is very much under the spell of Sternberg. The listed sources are two books, *A Century of Gunmen*, by Frederick Watson (London, 1931), and *The Saga of Billy the Kid*, by Walter Noble Burns (Garden City, 1926). Watson's book turns out not to yield a single fact; it is merely an entry in the bibliography. This opening, then, except for the information about Billy's age and the number of men he was reputed to have killed, is sheer invention. The phrase about 'not counting Mexicans' is even contrary to the historical record, for in real life Billy was a great intimate of Mexicans, families of whom often harboured him from the law. The killings Billy did not count were those of Indians. Here is the first instance of what Borges called 'the flagrant contradiction of my chosen authority.'

Now for the first chapter, 'The Larval Stage':

Along about 1859, the man who would become known to terror and glory as Billy the Kid was born in a cellar room of a New York city tenement. It is said that he was spawned by a tired-out Irish womb but was brought up among Negroes. In this tumult of lowly smells and woolly heads, he enjoyed a superiority that stemmed from having freckles and a mop of red hair. He took pride in being white; he was also scrawny, wild, and coarse. At the age of twelve, he fought in the gang of the Swamp Angels, that branch of divinities who operated among the neighborhood sewers. On nights redolent of burnt fog, they would clamber out of that foul-smelling labyrinth, trail some German sailor, do him in with a knock on the head, strip him to his underwear, and afterward sneak back to the filth of their starting place. Their leader was a gray-haired Negro, Gas House Jones, who was also celebrated as a poisoner of horses.

Sometimes, from the upper window of a waterfront dive, a woman would dump a bucket of ashes upon the head of a prospective victim. As he gasped and choked, Swamp Angels would swarm him, rush him into a cellar, and plunder him.

Such were the apprentice years of Billy Harrigan, the future Billy the Kid. Nor did he scorn the offerings of Bowery playhouses, enjoying in particular (perhaps without an inkling that they were signs and symbols of his destiny) cowboy melodramas.

To begin with, history's Billy was William H. Bonney, not Harrigan. Bonney was born in New York, in 1859, but nothing is known of his life there, for at the age of three his family emigrated to Kansas. Borges turned up another character named Billy the Kid in Herbert Asbury's *Gangs of New York*, the book

he used as the source of one of his other infamy stories, and he has grafted the two lives, thus providing
the famous Billy the Kid with a past. In this chapter,
all the details of the activities of the Swamp Angels
are lifted straight from Asbury.

The following brief chapter in Borges's account is
called 'Go West!':

If the jammed Bowery theaters (whose top-gallery riffraff shouted
'Hoist that rag!' when the curtain failed to rise promptly on
schedule) abounded in these blood and thunder productions,
the simple explanation is that America was then experiencing the lure of the Far West. Beyond the sunset lay the gold-
fields of Nevada and California. Beyond the sunset were the
redwoods, going down before the ax; the buffalo's huge Baby-
lonian face; Brigham Young's beaver hat and plural bed; the red
man's ceremonies and his rampages; the clear air of the deserts;
endless-stretching range land; and the earth itself, whose nearness quickens the heart like the nearness of the sea. The West
beckoned. A slow, steady rumor populated those years – that
of thousands of Americans taking possession of the West. On
that march, around 1872, was Bill Harrigan, treacherous as a
bull rattler, in flight from a rectangular cell.

Here the detail about Bowery theatres is from
Asbury and the bull rattler image from Burns. The
catalogue belongs to Borges; he calls the technique
'random enumeration', and it is one of the overly ex-
ploited tricks he talks about in his 1935 preface. The

idea itself comes from Whitman. Elsewhere, Borges remarked on the difficulty of

the setting down of a limited catalog of endless things. The task, as is evident, is impossible, for such chaotic enumeration can only be simulated, and every apparently haphazard element has to be linked to its neighbor either by secret association or by contrast.

The technique was employed in several of the pieces in both the first and third parts of *A Universal History of Infamy*, was used liberally in the later short stories, and, of course, reached perfection in a brilliant page of the story called 'The Aleph'.

Next comes the chapter 'The Demolition of a Mexican':

History (which, like certain film directors, proceeds by a series of abrupt images) now puts forward the image of a danger-filled saloon, located – as if on the high seas – out in the heart of the all-powerful desert. The time, a blustery night of the year 1873; the place, the Staked Plains of New Mexico. All around, the land is almost uncannily flat and bare, but the sky, with its storm-piled clouds and moon, is full of fissured cavities and mountains. There are a cow's skull, the howl and the eyes of coyotes in the shadows, trim horses, and from the saloon an elongated patch of light. Inside, leaning over the bar, a group of strapping but tired men drink a liquor that warms them for a fight; at the same time, they make a great show of large silver coins bearing a serpent and an eagle. A drunk croons to himself, poker-faced. Among the men are several who speak in a language with many s's, which must be Spanish, for those who speak it are looked down on. Bill Harrigan, the red-topped tenement rat, stands among the drinkers. He has downed a couple of *aguardientes* and thinks of asking for one more, maybe because he hasn't a cent left. He is somewhat overwhelmed by these men of the desert. He sees them as imposing, boisterous, happy, and hatefully wise in the handling of wild cattle and big horses. All at once there is dead silence, ignored only by the voice of the drunk, singing out of tune. Someone has come in – a big, burly Mexican, with the face of an old Indian squaw. He is endowed with an immense sombrero and with a pair of six-guns at his side. In awkward English he wishes a good evening to all the gringo sons of bitches who are drinking. Nobody takes up the challenge. Bill asks who he is, and they whisper to him, in fear, that the Dago – that is, the Diego – is Belisario Villagrán, from Chihuahua. At once, there is a resounding blast. Sheltered by that wall of tall men, Bill has fired at the intruder. The glass drops from Villagrán's hand; then the man himself drops. He does not need another bullet. Without deigning to glance at the showy dead man, Bill picks up his end of the conversation. 'Is that so?' he drawled. 'Well, I'm Billy the Kid, from New York.' The drunk goes on singing, unheeded.

One may easily guess the apotheosis. Bill gives out handshakes all around and accepts praises, cheers, and whiskeys. Someone notices that there are no notches on the handle of his revolver and offers to cut one to stand for Villagrán's death. Billy the Kid keeps this someone's razor, though he says that

'It's hardly worthwhile noting down Mexicans.' This, perhaps, is not quite enough. That night, Bill lays out his blanket beside the corpse and – with great show – sleeps till daybreak.

Here, again, the technique is cinematic, and the film director is Josef von Sternberg. The real Billy was dark-haired and not a redhead. The real Billy, according to Burns, killed his first man at the age of twelve, and he did so with a pocket-knife, not a bullet. Nor were the circumstances anything like the cold-blooded ones painted by Borges; only later on was Billy to kill as 'nonchalantly as he smoked a cigarette.' None of the events in this chapter ever took place, then, except in Borges's imagination.

Let's now turn to the final chapter, 'Deaths for Deaths' Sake':

Out of the lucky blast (at the age of fourteen), Billy the Kid the hero was born, and the furtive Bill Harrigan died. The boy of the sewer and the knock on the head rose to become a man of the frontier. He made a horseman of himself, learning to ride straight in the saddle – Wyoming- or Texas-style – and not with his body thrown back, the way they rode in Oregon and California. He never completely matched his legend, but he kept getting closer and closer to it. Something of the New York hoodlum lived on in the cowboy; he transferred to Mexicans the hate that had previously been inspired in him by Negroes, but the last words he ever spoke were (swear) words in Spanish. He learned another, more difficult art – how to lead men. Both helped to make him a good cattle rustler. From time to time, Old Mexico's guitars and whorehouses pulled on him.

With the haunting lucidity of insomnia, he organized populous orgies that often lasted four days and four nights. In the end, glutted, he settled accounts with bullets. While his trigger finger was unfailing, he was the most feared man (and perhaps the most anonymous and most lonely) of that whole frontier. Pat Garrett, his friend, the sheriff who later killed him, once told him, 'I've had a lot of practice with the rifle shooting buffalo.'

'I've had plenty with the six-shooter,' Billy replied modestly. 'Shooting tin cans and men.'

The details can never be recovered, but it is known that he was credited with up to twenty-one killings – 'not counting Mexicans.' For seven desperate years, he practiced the extravagance of utter recklessness.

The night of the twenty-fifth of July 1880, Billy the Kid came galloping on his piebald down the main, or only, street of Fort Sumner. The heat was oppressive and the lamps had not been lighted; Sheriff Garrett, seated on a porch in a rocking chair, drew his revolver and sent a bullet through the kid's belly. The horse kept on; the rider tumbled into the dust of the road. Garrett got off a second shot. The townspeople (knowing the wounded man was Billy the Kid) locked their window shutters tight. The agony was long and blasphemous. In the morning, the sun by then high overhead, they began drawing near, and they disarmed him. The man was gone. They could see in his face that used-up look of the dead.

He was shaved, sheathed in ready-made clothes, and displayed to awe and ridicule in the window of Fort Sumner's biggest store. Men on horseback and in buckboards gathered from miles and miles around. On the third day, they had to use make-up on him. On the fourth day, he was buried with rejoicing.

Only the exchange with Garrett about shooting tin cans and men has its source in Burns. The rest is made up. Just how much Borges departed from the facts can be demonstrated by comparing his version of Billy's death with the account of it given in *The Saga of Billy the Kid*. There, we are told that Billy had been tracked by Garrett and two deputies to Fort Sumner, where they were questioning the Kid's friend Pete Maxwell about him. It was around midnight, and a full moon was in the sky. Garrett was in Pete's darkened bedroom, waking him. The two deputies squatted and smoked on the porch outside. Billy suddenly appeared from a house next door, where he had gone for a late supper, and he walked innocently into their midst. Bootless and coatless, he was carrying a kitchen knife, having come to carve himself a steak from a beef that hung on Maxwell's porch. When he saw the men he whipped out his revolver and asked, *'¿Quién es?'* He did not suspect that they were deputies, otherwise he would have fired. Instead, he ducked indoors, into Pete Maxwell's room, and asked Pete, again in Spanish, who the men outside were. Garrett, sitting by Pete's bed, reached for his gun. The Kid noticed the movement and called out again, '*¿Quién es?*' But Garrett dropped down and answered the question with a shot. Billy fell dead with a bullet through his heart. Garrett got off a second shot that was later found imbedded in the underside of a table. Then, writes Burns,

They carried the body across the Maxwell yard into a deserted carpenter shop, full of dust and cobwebs, its floor littered with shavings, and laid it on an old work bench. The town was aroused by now. Excited Mexican men and women gathered at the scene and crowded into the shop....

Bringing candles, the women lighted them about the body. In the shine of the candles, the Kid lay all night in rude state, the dusty work bench for his bier. And all night the women in their black dresses, with their black *rebozos* about their heads, crouched along the walls of the dim, dingy room, weeping.

The date was 15 July 1881 – nearly a year after the date Borges gave. 'The hearse was a rickety old wagon drawn by a pair of scrawny Mexican ponies,' Burns goes on.

Not six people were left in Fort Sumner during the funeral. The entire population, men, women, and children, turned out to do the Kid last honours and followed his corpse to the little military cemetery a short distance east of town. A stranger might have thought the funeral that of Fort Sumner's most distinguished citizen.

Had Borges not introduced the name Billy the Kid at all, we might never have suspected his story of being anything other than an original creation. But in that case the piece would have amounted to little more than 'a surface of images', for it is only as an alternative life of Billy the Kid that the story has a deeper significance. What Borges's Billy is about – what Borges at his best is about – is the nature of what we can know, of appearance and reality. This, the Berkeleyan notion that reality is perceived with the mind and that its interpretation is relative to the percipient, is very much what underlies the story. (Let us recall that to Borges the eighteenth-century Irish metaphysician was 'one of the most lovable men in the whole history of philosophy.') Whitman once remarked that he was 'afraid of the historians: the historian, if not a liar himself, is largely at the mercy of liars.' The ideas have a kinship. If history is not the past but images of the past and if these images are dependent upon any individual's memory, Borges's particular selection and arrangement of events is as valid as anyone else's. By extension, his life of Billy the Kid becomes a parody of history, a parody of biography. It is a game and more than a game. It becomes, finally, a stance that fits the basic scepticism long acknowledged by Borges as his view of life.

There is no need here to go into the other six infamy pieces and to detail page by page the correspondences and discrepancies with the credited sources.* The discussion of 'The Disinterested Killer Bill Harrigan' was an attempt to show that Borges's originality resides in his departure from and in his compression and transformation of given factual information – in other words, in the free use he makes of his source material to create something new.

Five other infamy stories follow this same pattern, some more, some less. A sixth piece, however, 'The Insulting Master of Etiquette Kôtsuké no Suké', a tale of eighteenth-century Japanese samurai, is hardly more than a retelling in a few pages of the twenty-three-page narrative called 'The Forty-seven Rónins' from A.B. Mitford's *Tales of Old Japan*. Of the five with the same pattern as the biography of Billy the Kid, there is one with qualities that are altogether unique. This is the seventh and final infamy story, called 'The Masked Dyer, Hakim of Merv'. The tale demands singling out for further discussion.

It had long been suspected by scholars and by translators that something was wrong about the sources that Borges gave for his piece on Hakim, the Veiled Prophet of Khurasan. One of them, Sir Percy Sykes's *History of Persia*, yields a small paragraph of ten or so lines that tell nothing vital; the other, the puzzling German work *Die Vernichtung der Rose*, by Alexander Schulz, no one had ever been able to lay hands

---

* For this, see below, 'A Footnote to Infamy', pp. 233–49.

on. As far back as 1958, after having run through the one source and complained about the inaccessibility of the other, Roger Caillois, an early French translator of Borges, suggested in an afterword to his version of *A Universal History of Infamy* that the Hakim story was 'entirely original', but, unable to confirm this, he qualified his statement twice over – first, by saying that Borges's text 'appears to be entirely original', then by concluding, 'I do not wish to prejudice whatever conclusions may be reached by a deeper and more extensive study.' Clearly, Caillois lacked the courage of his conviction, and we are left unconvinced by his conjecture. His suspicions, of course, were completely correct. The piece is a hoax; it is the first of a long line of Borges hoaxes. Not until Borges and I translated the story together back in the Argentine winter of 1971 was the truth about 'Hakim of Merv' revealed to me. Here is the story of how I stumbled on the discovery.

Months before I translated a single word of *A Universal History of Infamy*, I began collecting copies of the books Borges had listed as his sources. Several of them were still in his library. He promptly made me a gift of them, along with a handful of others that he had bought and read in the early 1930s with an eye to culling for additional sketches. In none of these volumes had Borges left a single mark to give a clue to his use of them. So I read and annotated, and the detective work crept along. My concern, since all the sources except for that German puzzler, were in English, was not to blunder ahead and translate from Spanish into English what had, to begin with, been translated by Borges from English into Spanish. To give each piece the required flavour, I wanted to see exactly the words and phrases Borges had either translated straight or transformed into something else. Armed and primed in this way, I one day went to him, ready to tackle 'Hakim of Merv'. I told him there was nothing in Sykes's history, and I began pressing about the German work. Since I had found no trace of it among his books, I was suspicious. Its full citation reads: '*Die Vernichtung der Rose*, nach dem arabischen Urtext übertragen von Alexander Schulz. Leipzig, 1927.' – meaning, 'The Annihilation of the Rose, translated from the Arabic by Alexander Schulz', etc. In a challenging tone, I said, 'And this German work by Alexander Schulz...?' and then I stopped in mid-sentence. It had come to me that this was his old friend, the painter and mystic Xul Solar, and that the attribution was indeed made up. Yes, Borges confirmed, the whole piece was an invention, sources and all. Alexander Schulz stood for Alejandro Schulz Solari, or as he was commonly called, Xul Solar. 'And no one has known for forty years?' I asked. 'No,' Borges said, 'not for certain, and we mustn't spoil the joke by letting the cat out of the bag.'

In retrospect, it is all so obvious. I suppose what had baffled Caillois was the deception put forward in the book's 1954 preface about distorting 'the tales of others.' When we examine the erudition of the story's first page, Borges's authorship becomes plain. The tale opens:

If I am not mistaken, the chief sources of information concerning Mokanna, the Veiled (or, literally, Masked) Prophet of Khurasan, are only four in number: a) those passages from the *History of the Caliphs* culled by Baladhuri; b) the *Giant's Handbook*, or *Book of Precision and Revision*, by the official historian of the Abbasids, Ibn abi Tahir Taifur; c) the Arabic codex entitled *The Annihilation of the Rose*, wherein we find a refutation of the abominable heresies of the *Dark Rose*, which was the Prophet's holy book; and d) some barely legible coins unearthed by the engineer Andrusov during excavations for the Trans-Caspian Railway. These coins, now on deposit in the Numismatic Collection at Tehran, preserve certain Persian distichs which abridge or emend key passages of the *Annihilation*. The original *Rose* is lost, for the manuscript found in 1899 and published all too hastily in the *Morganländisches Archiv* has been pronounced a forgery – first by Horn and afterward by Sir Percy Sykes.

In his foreword to *In Praise of Darkness*, dated 1969, Borges listed certain rules that he had been following over the years, among them,

to work into a story circumstantial details, which readers now insist on; [and] to feign slight uncertainties, for, although reality is exact, memory is not....

The opening paragraph of 'Hakim of Merv' is crammed with circumstantial details – nearly all bogus, of course. Four books, one journal, and no less than six authorities are cited. As for the slight uncertainties, there are several. All these are Borges hallmarks. Compare the passage with the apocryphal erudition that appears in the second paragraph of the celebrated hoax 'The Approach to al-Mu'tasim', which was originally published in 1936 in a collection of Borges's essays:

> The first edition of *The Approach to al-Mu'tasim* appeared in Bombay towards the end of 1932. The paper on which the volume was issued, I am told, was almost newsprint; the jacket announced to the purchaser that the book was the first detective novel to be written by a native of Bombay City. Within a few months, four printings of a thousand copies each were sold out. The *Bombay Quarterly Review*, the *Bombay Gazette*, the *Calcutta Review*, the *Hindustani Review* (of Allahabad), and the *Calcutta Englishman* all sang its praises. Bahadur then brought out an illustrated edition, which he retitled *The Conversation with the Man Called al-Mu'tasim* and rather beautifully subtitled *A Game with Shifting Mirrors*. This is the edition which Victor Gollancz has just reissued in London, with a foreword by Dorothy L. Sayers and the omission – perhaps merciful – of the illustrations.

And this from the beginning of 'Death and the Compass' (1942):

[Lönnrot] pointed to a row of tall books on a shelf in the closet. There were a *Vindication of Robert Fludd*, a literal translation of the *Sefer Yeçirah*, a *Biography of the Baal Shem*, a *History of the Hasidic Sect*, a treatise (in German) on the Tetragrammaton, and another on the names of God in the Pentateuch.

All three passages are full of irony and bookish jokes. Borges never failed to roar with laughter over the outlandish title *Giant's Handbook* and its sub-title, *Book of Precision and Revision*. 'How precise can it have been in the first place,' he once said to me, 'if it required revision?' As for the Bombay detective novel that sold so well its author retitled and repackaged it, one can hear Borges chuckling over the links with Victor Gollancz, a real London publisher, and Dorothy L. Sayers, a real writer of detective fiction. Borges often told the story of his great friend Bioy Casares being taken in and trying to order the book from London – though this may be apocryphal too. In the rabbi's library, the book called a *Vindication of the Kabbalah* is the same title as an essay by Borges himself, written eleven years earlier.

This combination of sham erudition, of real authors mixed with spurious titles, and all of it just saved from priggishness by the humour (in some of Borges's early essays, where the erudition is real, the priggishness is fatal), is found in story after story and collection after collection. It is in nearly every one of the seventeen tales that make up *Ficciones*;

it is somewhat curbed but nonetheless frequent in the seventeen stories of *El Aleph*. It is also present in numerous passages of *The Book of Imaginary Beings* and throughout the *Chronicles of Bustos Domecq*. Sham erudition is perhaps the most consistent and characteristic mark of Borges's fiction – of the strain of his fiction that won him his international fame. But Borges, who feared imitating himself when he returned to storywriting in the late 1960s, no longer relied on his hallmark in the last two collections or in his last four stories, although inevitably some traces of it remain. The feature, then, was essayed in 'The Masked Dyer, Hakim of Merv', Borges's first truly Borgesian story.

A couple of other things are worth pointing out in this story. In its sixth part, 'The Abominable Mirrors', we are treated to the tenets of the prophet Hakim's personal creed. These are sheer invention, of course – or, as we shall see, sheer invention with a special Borges twist. 'At the root of Hakim's cosmogony,' wrote Borges,

is a spectral god. This godhead is as majestically devoid of origin as of name or face. It is an unchanging god, but its image cast nine shadows which, condescending to creation, conceived and presided over a first heaven. Out of this first demiurgic crown there issued a second, with its own angels, powers, and thrones, and these founded a lower heaven, which was the symmetrical mirror of the first. This second conclave, in its turn, was mirrored in a third, and this in a lower one, and so on to the number 999. The lord of this lowermost heaven is he who rules us – shadow of shadows of still other shadows – and his fraction of divinity approaches zero.

What Borges was attempting here is the first seed of what he was to develop several years later in his most ambitious short story, 'Tlön, Uqbar, Orbis Tertius', in which he projects a whole alternative world. As for the twist, it lies in the fact that Borges introduced Hakim's cosmogony by telling us that in the prophet's creed 'borrowings from old Gnostic beliefs are nonetheless detectable.' Of course they are, because Borges lifted Hakim's cosmogony – except for one small detail – from the Gnostic cosmogony of Basilides. What Borges was doing, in effect, was making fun of Hakim for having cribbed from the Gnostics and at the same time making fun of himself, since in reality it was he, Borges, who had done the cribbing. What is more, the filching comes from an essay of his own, 'A Vindication of the False Basilides', written in 1931. There, in its second paragraph, we read: 'At the root of Basilides' cosmogony is a god. This godhead is as majestically devoid of name as of origin', etc. Only two things are different about the passage in the essay; it contains a sentence and a half that are deleted in the story version, and it numbers the heavens as 365 and not 999.

Next in Hakim's cosmogony comes this passage:

The world in which we live is a mistake, a clumsy parody. Mirrors and fatherhood, because they multiply and confirm the parody, are abominations.

The second sentence here appears identically in 'Tlön, Uqbar, Orbis Tertius', where it has become famous and where Borges attributed it to a page of *The Anglo-American Cyclopaedia*.

Roger Caillois, in his speculations on the sources of 'Hakim of Merv', makes use of an early text translated from the Arabic, parts of which found their way into an eighteenth-century French encyclopedia. But I suspect that Borges took whatever background he needed for his story from the pages of the *Encyclopædia Britannica*, whose Eleventh Edition came into his possession around 1929 or so. There, in Volume V, we find a sixty-two-column article on 'Caliphates', written by a Dutch scholar. In another volume are several extensive pieces on 'Mahomet' and related topics. Even the eleven-line entry, in Volume XVIII, on 'Mokanna' is a more worthwhile résumé than the discussion of similar length in Sykes. A close look at this edition of the *Britannica* will also reveal certain close stylistic affinities between Borges and his favourite encyclopedia. No one to my knowledge has taken up such a line of investigation.

As for the middle part of *A Universal History of Infamy*, the short story 'Streetcorner Man', we need not dwell long on it. About Buenos Aires low-life and knife fighters, it represents a second strain in Borges's work, which, although interesting, would never have brought him greatness on its own. I do not particularly prize this side of Borges. (My view is entirely personal. Male prowess of the kind he seemed to admire is embedded in a worship of barbarism still prevalent among many of his countrymen. It was a trait he recognized in them and one with which I – after half a lifetime's attachment to the Argentine – am still unable to reconcile myself.) And yet a reviewer writing in the Boston *Globe* once accused me of having unleashed in Borges an interest in gangsters and the *demi-monde*. A case of deduction gone awry, the logic ran as follows: a) Borges had stopped composing short stories until di Giovanni came along and made him start writing again; b) *Doctor Brodie's Report*, six of whose eleven stories are about knife fights, is the result of the Borges–di Giovanni collaboration; ergo, c) di G. made Borges write about knives.

'Streetcorner Man' is the prototype of all these stories, but when it first appeared in print in Buenos Aires, in 1933, I had not yet begun my collaboration with Borges. In fact, the tale beat me into this world – a continent away in Newton, Massachusetts – by seventeen days. Of his story, Borges said that

out of shyness, and perhaps a feeling that the story was a bit beneath me, I signed it with a pen name…. Although the story became popular to the point of embarrassment (today I only find it stagy and mannered and the characters bogus), I never regarded it as a starting point. It simply stands there as a kind of freak.

Indeed, in atonement for the story's excesses, Borges wrote a sequel to it in 1969. He described the new story, 'Rosendo's Tale', as 'a fair rendering of what actually happened, or might have happened, in an early and all-too-famous extravaganza of mine called "Streetcorner Man". In the new version I have done my best to hark back to sanity.' This says it all.

The 'Etcetera' pieces of the third and final section of *A Universal History of Infamy* are also worth comparing with their sources. Once again, the real source and the listed source do not exactly correspond. Several of the pieces are apocryphal, having been made up by Borges. The most important of these is 'The Mirror of Ink', which is yet another hoax. Here we come across a prototype Aleph dreamed up by Borges twelve years before he wrote his famous story about the magical object discovered by Carlos Argentino Daneri in a cellar in Calle Garay, in Buenos Aires. Such cross-pollination we have come to recognize as an artifice typical of Borges.

A Universal History of Infamy should be seen as seminal to the best of the stories that came after it. *Ficciones* and *The Aleph* are Borges's undoubted masterpieces. If the latter is the flower of his work,

A Universal History of Infamy is surely the embryo.
And here, in embryo form, along with the universal misappropriation of sources, are the mirrors and
fatherhood that – to our eternal delight – multiply
and confirm the element of parody in Borges's subsequent work.

Borges and His Autobiography

It would never have occurred to Jorge Luis Borges to set down in his own words the story of his life. In his view, the great adventure of his existence – and the only one he regarded as worthy of interest – lay in the books he read. Borges made it plain that he was not a man of action. He also made it plain that before he considered himself a poet or a prose writer he was 'first and foremost' a reader. Certainly he was never greedy for money and self-promotion, and as for fame or immortality his highest hope was that a few of his pages might survive. In terms of an account of his own life, his ideal – as he once confessed to me – was a piece of work in the nature of Coleridge's *Biographia Literaria*.

Borges's affinities with Coleridge are intriguing. Both men, avid and far-ranging readers, possessed speculative and inquiring minds; both sought out constant intellectual stimulus; both concerned themselves with the power of the imagination. But, in charting the evolution of his thought, Coleridge wrote a vast, sprawling work that has been universally hailed for its genius while it has also been criticized as 'maddeningly unsystematic in structure' and further characterized as 'one of the most annoying books in any language.' Coleridge's account of his life was written at the age of forty-three; Borges's at seventy. An element that these personal histories have in common is that each was written when its author was in desperately low spirits and, because of an upheaval in his private life, lacking in self-confidence.

There the connections end. Borges's autobiography, a far more modest undertaking, was written for an immediate editorial consideration that had nothing to do with a private inner compulsion. The essay was prompted by me, in fact, and then written by us directly in English. By 1970, we had finished work on the first two of a projected ten or twelve volumes of Borges's work in our collaborative translation. Borges was now increasingly eager to provide an English-speaking readership with some of his best older stories in the versions that we were then making and that were receiving acclaim in the pages of the *New Yorker* magazine. Our original idea had been to translate his book *The Aleph*, but the English-language rights to certain of the stories in that volume were denied us, despite Borges's pleas to several publishers and other interested parties. None would accede to his request; eventually, in anger, Borges named and slated one of these people in print, referring ironically to the man's 'unselfish and unswerving efforts … on our behalf' – by which, of course, Borges meant just the opposite. Our own generous New York publisher, however, undaunted by the setback, wrote to us to say he would be only too happy to publish a wide-ranging collection of stories that would provide at the same time the showcase we wanted for our work. But Borges and I were reluctant to bring out yet another anthology of his writings in English – his third. It was at this point, in order to provide something new and fresh, something that previous selections of Borges's work lacked, that I hit on the idea of a brief account of his life.

In travelling about the United States with him to different universities, I had noted that the great excitement and interest which readers showed in his work were often accompanied by an equally great misunderstanding and bewilderment. To Americans, Borges seemed to have come out of thin air, without a cultural past or background. A simple history of his life, it therefore occurred to me – one that would serve as a setting for the work – would help English-speaking readers grasp Borges's enigmatic tales and enable them to see how rooted his writing is in Argentine experience. The problem, however, was Borges, who had always regarded it as immodest and found it notoriously difficult to speak about himself or his own work in public. But in the United States, I had long since noted that no matter what subject he spoke on in the lecture hall – Cervantes or Shakespeare, classic Argentine authors or Keats – Borges was afterwards invariably bombarded from the floor with questions about his own stories or poems. He always replied straightforwardly, unhesitantly, illuminatingly, and – what was more – he took enormous pleasure in doing so. It gratified him to find his work being read widely and carefully. The difficulty, I saw, would be in helping to guide him away from the pitfalls of extemporaneous speech to a finished, structured piece of writing.

An opportunity seemed to arise at the end of 1969, when the University of Oklahoma invited Borges to deliver a series of lectures over a generous three-week period. As we prepared the programme, I somehow managed to convince him that, along with the lectures he wanted to give on Argentine writers of the past, he should include a talk about himself. I left it at that. I could never have persuaded him that an American audience was more interested in Jorge Luis Borges than in figures like Jose Hernández, Leopoldo Lugones, or Macedonio Fernández.

On the afternoon he was to deliver it, this lecture became an ordeal for Borges; he was in an absolute panic. Three times we circumnavigated the block in Norman, Oklahoma, where our hotel was located, as I helped him to rehearse. It was just as he describes having once done on a similar occasion years earlier in Adrogué with his mother. In the end, his performance was a success. Remembering this several months later, when we were committed to filling out a volume of his stories with some brand-new material, I wrote to the university and asked them for a transcript of the lecture. In due course, it arrived – all twenty pages of it. My idea had been to expand the text by another ten pages. Instead, when the typescript arrived, I found to my horror that it leapt about so nervously from topic to topic and was so tangled in tracking back and forth in time that the material was positively unhelpful. I dreaded having to tell Borges this. On the day that he and I sat down at the National Library to start, I made the uneasy announcement that we would not get much out of the Oklahoma transcript. Without a second thought or a murmur of disappointment or chagrin, Borges told me we should fling the pages aside and begin anew.

Before writing a word we talked over a scheme. The Oklahoma script had shown me that the story of his life must be outlined and then carefully guided to stick to a written plan. Borges agreed. I suggested we set down a simple list of topics – where he was born, his father's family, his mother's – and start from these. He agreed. At some point, I suggested a division into chapters, and I even titled them, hoping they would serve as mileposts. In the end, all that the lecture yielded was half of one sentence. Our new version, when we finished it, was more than double the length of our early projection.

The autobiography tells of Borges's protected childhood in Buenos Aires during the early years of the last century. The chief element in his life, his father's library, firmly set the pattern for an exclusively literary life. Borges *père* was an admirer of the English poets, an enthusiasm he passed on to his son. In 1914 came the family's long residence abroad in Geneva and in Spain, years in which Borges was educated in French and also learned German. (His English was nearly native; his father's mother, with whom he grew up, was from Staffordshire.) In Europe, Borges began to write and to frequent literary circles. In 1921, returning to rediscover Buenos Aires, he immediately became one of Argentina's leading avant-garde poets. A fury of work ensued – essays, poems, and reviews – most of it later repudiated or heavily rewritten. Then, in the late 1930s, almost surreptitiously, came the prose fiction that decades later made his international fame. At the same time, illness and blindness came to give shape to his ascetic character and ironic attitudes. His later years, before the final decline, show us a self-effacing, mischievous Borges, a man who knows his own foibles.

The story Borges does not tell is that of the long series of star-crossed relationships with women – all unforgettable, all forgotten, as he once summed them up – and the attraction he had for society belles, many of them dabblers in literature. The forewords he wrote to their books were a joke in Buenos

Aires. A preface by Borges, it was said, was the kiss of death.

There is some idea that Borges dictated his autobiography (in English, of course) and that I simply took down his words. As all the writing of the last two decades of his life was dictated (I speak of his solo work, not of what he wrote with Adolfo Bioy Casares and others), I feel a distinction must be made between the way we composed the story of his life and what was typed for him by a long series of secretaries. These secretaries functioned as machines, and Borges was glad of it. He once told an audience in New York that one of them was so uncritical that she put down all his slips rather than silently correct them. She even recorded his punctuation by writing down 'full stop' or 'semicolon'. This was true; I had pointed it out to him myself. But he felt quite safe, he went on to say, because he couldn't make a fool of himself with her.

I seldom took down any dictation from him in Spanish. When he said of our collaborative efforts, 'We don't think of ourselves as two men when we are working. We are two minds attempting the same goal', he was referring to our work in English. He was secure and comfortable in the knowledge that I would guide and shape his use of English, silently, or, when necessary, explicitly. He also knew, after two years of our collaboration, that what we were doing functioned only because we could each be openly frank and critical without hurting the other's feelings. Ingratiation was out of the question. Asked on one occasion about how he operated with Bioy, Borges said:

... we do not think of ourselves as two friends or even two writers; we just try to evolve a story. When somebody asks me, 'Did that sentence come from your side of the table or the other?' I can't tell him.

He went on to say that he and I worked in the same spirit; and we did. To get the autobiography started I dictated its first sentence, which Borges then pounced on and orally revised. I did not have to scribble, because we proceeded slowly, shaping our sentences aloud before anything was recorded on the page. Once things were flowing, I could often anticipate him and if he ran dry I would pick up the thread, speak out, and take down my own dictation. When our sessions finished, the notebook I wrote in came home with me, and I typed our words onto a fresh page and then set about checking facts and dates. 'What was the name of the ship you returned to Buenos Aires on in 1921?' 'It was the beginning of 1921, but I don't remember the ship's name. Ask my mother.' Could I rely on the memory of a woman in her nineties? I questioned doña Leonor about when the ship landed. 'It was the *Reina Victoria Eugenia*, and it was in March.' Not content with that, I ransacked the smelly old pages of the shipping news in newspapers in the filthy basement of the National Library. Sure enough, at the end of March that year a ship of that name had docked in the port of Buenos Aires.

All along I kept drawing Borges out, kept feeding him information, and most of all kept a rein on his digressions. There were two sections of the autobiography I was most pleased to have wormed out of him. Both were personal, and one was particularly touching. I had never read anywhere else or heard him tell anyone else what we wrote of his true opinion of certain works of his – three suppressed books of essays – of the 1920s. The same with the humiliating experience of his job in a lowly branch of the public library in the 1940s, when the whole of Argentina seemed to be plunged into bleak decay and moral chaos. 'I stuck out the library for about nine years,' he told me. 'They were nine years of solid unhappiness.... Sometimes in the evening, as I walked the ten blocks to the tramline, my eyes would be filled with tears.' I had a lump in my throat myself when he made this confession. To prompt these recollections, I had asked him to describe his daily life during this period. Borges baulked and said he could not see what bearing that had on anything, nor did he see what interest it would hold for anyone. If it interested me, it would interest our readers, I told him. After all, he was doing his finest work in those years. He relented without another word. I was gladdened, for I still regard these passages as the piece's best and certainly most moving pages.

The only argument we ever had came while we were writing about the suppressed books of essays. I wanted him to discuss them and to say why he had never allowed them back into print. Angry, Borges said no, he wanted to forget all about these 'unmentionables'. I was thinking about the shape of our piece; about its potential readers. How could we just skip over five or six years of his life? 'Why not?' he challenged me. 'Whose life is this?' Still determined, I took another tack. I didn't mind if he condemned the books, I told him, but I thought he had to speak of them. I read back to him what he had told me about these essay collections some days earlier. He liked what he heard and said he would mention the books if he could leave their titles out. That would make a fine touch, I thought; it would underline his condemnation of them. I wholeheartedly agreed.

At one point in his story, Borges relates an amusing anecdote about the novel, *El caudillo*, which his father completed in Majorca, in 1921:

He had some five hundred copies of the book printed, and brought them back to Buenos Aires, where he gave them away to friends. Every time the word 'Paraná – his home town – came up in the manuscript, the printers had changed it to 'Panamá', thinking they were correcting a mistake. Not to give

them trouble, and also seeing that it was funnier that way, my
father let this pass.

I wanted to verify all this, and Borges's mother
obliged me with a battered copy of her husband's
novel. There I found the word 'Paraná' spelled correctly
at least half a dozen times, so I assumed Borges had
made the story up. I said nothing to him. It was funny,
and if this was the way he wanted to tell it – or wanted
to remember it – that was fine with me. It was, as he
said, his life. But looking into *El caudillo* again almost
thirty years after the episode I am recounting, I find a
detail that had previously escaped me. On p. 126, the
word in question appears in hybrid form as 'Paramá' –
sufficient proof that the little story is at least half true.

One small anomaly in the text may be worth
pointing out. In the last page or two, describing
the lineage of a long story he was then engaged in
writing, Borges refers obliquely and laconically to
an unnamed spouse. ('Finally, as I was telling [the
plot] to my wife ...') The mention of such a partner,
when no marriage had been spoken of, was not good
editorial usage. I knew this, but wishing just then to
spare Borges the pain any elucidation might cause,
I let the lapse pass. Not so the *New Yorker*'s editors,
who, in their proofsheets, asked me to 'explain her
& when he married'. Explain I did, and at the same
time I pleaded for a dispensation. I even provided alternative wording, should my plea fail. But exemption

was granted. The woman, of course, was Elsa Astete Millán, whom Borges had married in 1967.

On the first afternoon, we drafted five pages. But soon our efforts slowed to a snail's pace. Borges was in the midst of a painful legal separation (there was no divorce in Argentina at the time) and found it difficult to concentrate, often for days on end. On many afternoons, we were unable to write a single word. On some days we managed a short paragraph. What at the outset I thought would take us two weeks extended to over three months. The important thing, however, was that as the work developed Borges enjoyed it. Early on I sent the first chapter to the *New Yorker* (with which we were under contract for any new writing that Borges produced), and they assured us that if the piece continued in a similar vein they would publish it. Borges was heartened. When it first appeared, in the issue of 19 September 1970 (it reappeared in book form a few months later in *The Aleph and Other Stories 1933–1969*), the autobiography was a literary sensation in New York. Soon after, the work came out in Brazil, in a Portuguese translation, and then in both German and Italian versions. Although French translation rights were acquired in 1971, the essay did not appear in that language until 1980. (I always surmised that Borges's unflattering remarks about the French language, and his disdain for certain aspects of French literary life, 'its fondness for schools and movements' and 'its literary cliques that wallowed in publicity and bickering', had been responsible for the delay.) Within days of the essay's appearance in the *New Yorker*, a Barcelona publisher wrote to us for permission to publish the piece as a book in a Spanish translation. At the same time, *La Nación*, the Buenos Aires daily, offered its pages.

On each of these occasions, Borges baulked. It was then that he mentioned Coleridge's *Biographia Literaria* to me. He also confessed that he had qualms about the amount of documentation – dates – the piece contained. Something about this, which I did not understand at the time, troubled him. We simply let the matter drop. It was not until ten or twelve years later, when I was translating into English his life of Evaristo Carriego, that I at last began to understand Borges's reservations. In his Carriego book, Borges was trying to write about a man's essence, or eternity, by means of 'a timeless description' that would eschew any manner of 'chronological account'. Certainly no other biography that I know of is so stripped bare of dates. If memory serves me, there are only six in the whole book. What Borges had wanted for Carriego in 1930 was to seek the pattern of his life; what he wanted for himself in 1970 was a Coleridgean account of the evolution of his thought. What I had felt English-speaking readers needed at the time was a narrative of Borges's life firmly grounded in everyday detail. I think we were both right, each in his own way. For Borges's taste – for a Coleridge-style version of his life, for his eternity – we have, of course, the many volumes of Borges's written works and his conversations.

The essence of his life Borges regarded as his reading. As early as 1935, he said that 'Sometimes I suspect that good readers are even blacker and rarer swans than good writers.... Reading, obviously, is an activity which comes after that of writing; it is more modest, more unobtrusive, more intellectual.' These words were perhaps his true epitaph. For my part, I still find him and his gentle wisdom in the pages of his autobiography, where, despite a large share of personal adversity – blindness and sexual failures – his determination to find happiness shines through on every page. 'At my age, one should be aware of one's limits,' he said,

and this knowledge may make for happiness. When I was young, I thought of literature as a game of skilled and surprising variations; now that I have found my own voice, I feel that tinkering and tampering neither greatly improve nor greatly spoil my drafts.... As to failure or fame, they are quite irrelevant and I never bother about them. What I'm out for now is peace, the enjoyment of thinking and of friendship, and, though it may be too ambitious, a sense of loving and of being loved.

How I wish the story of Borges's autobiography could have ended on this happy note. But it is uncanny the way Borges's fictional concern with the multiplication and corruption of texts has come to haunt him in real life. The essay went out of print some time ago in English; then, a few years back, it occurred to me that the piece might make a useful small book combined with a memoir of mine about my working relationship with Borges which was published in 1988 and which had also gone out of print. An Argentine publisher expressed interest in the project. In due course, the Borges Estate granted permission for the half-share it controlled in the autobiography, but a stipulation was made that my memoir not be included in the volume. After delays of nearly a year, María Kodama – Borges's last companion and the woman to whom he left all his intellectual property – with the approval of the Estate's lawyer, signed a contract. No sooner had she done so, however, than she changed her mind, thereby unleashing on three continents an almost comical *brouhaha* that has come to involve a whole battery of publishers, agents, editors, translators, reviewers, gossipmongers, and lawyers.

Ultimately, a version of the autobiography appeared in Buenos Aires in April 1999, but editorial haste and chaos – to describe matters in the kindest possible light – combined to mar Marcial Souto's impeccable translation of the work. An overzealous Argentine editor somehow took it upon himself to pepper the text with stylistic infelicities, typographical liberties, and

factual errors. At the same time, the book's publisher
denied the translator and me a meaningful opportunity to see proofs. I had also been asked for a foreword, but at the last moment the publishers decided
not to print it, lest any further hand of mine in the
book arouse Kodama's wrath. Borges deserved better than this in his own country and on the eve of
the centenary of his birth. (I believe I can speak for
Souto, who consulted me closely during the course
of his work, when I say we repudiate the unfortunate Buenos Aires text.) Meanwhile, also early in
1999, while one Barcelona publisher was negotiating
with me to publish a Spanish edition of the autobiography in Souto's unpolluted version, another
Barcelona publisher, dealing with Kodama, commissioned an amateurish translation of the same
work, to which Kodama contributed a memoir of
her own.

When the alarm bells went off, the second publishing house drew me into the negotiations but
carefully neglected to mention that their book was
already printed and bound and ready for distribu-
tion. Leaping into the ensuing dispute, the Spanish
press and assorted hacks were quick to take sides. A
member of the Spanish Royal Academy – or possibly
Borges's H. Bustos Domecq posing as a member of
the Spanish Royal Academy – announced in his review of the Argentine edition of the book that what
had first appeared in the *New Yorker* in 1970 was

not a work written in English but a translation by me from the Spanish, and that Souto's version was a re-translation back into Spanish. Eschewing all logic and common sense, the man failed to offer a clue as to the present whereabouts of the purported Spanish original. Livid at certain statements in the Buenos Aires dust-jacket blurb, our Spanish Bustos said it was inconceivable that I could have collaborated with Borges and, as the jacket had put it, guided him in writing the autobiography. 'Allow me to protest at this surprising piece of pretension that anyone could "guide" Borges', the reviewer fumed, ignorant of the fact that Borges must have been one the most guided people who ever lived. Among his guides – to mention only a few – had been his mother, his friend Adolfo Bioy Casares, his housemaid Fanny Uveda, María Kodama, and, for several years, me.

A few months later, another Spanish journalist, writing in *El País*, of Madrid, explained that the autobiography was a text 'read as a lecture at the University of Oklahoma in 1970'. Apparently, this was the silly season among newspapermen in Spain. First, the date, 1970, is mistaken; second, the talk delivered in Oklahoma was not the text in question, which was not written until many months later; third, if this text had been read, who read it (Borges was blind)?; and fourth, if the text had been given as a lecture it would have lasted for over three hours. That's a lot of misinformation in a mere eleven words.

All this reminds me of an anecdote Borges told about his story 'The Aleph':

Once, in Madrid, a journalist asked me whether Buenos Aires actually possessed an Aleph. I nearly yielded to temptation and said yes, but a friend broke in and pointed out that were such an object to exist it would not only be the most famous thing in the world but would also renew our whole conception of time, astronomy, mathematics, and space. 'Ah,' said the journalist, 'so the entire thing is your own invention. I thought it was true because you gave the name of the street.' I did not dare tell him that the naming of streets is not much of a feat.

Kodama herself, in her role since 1986 as keeper of the flame, seems fond of telling people that I stole the autobiography from Borges. By which I can only guess she means that I added commas to the Oklahoma transcript and then put my name to the result alongside Borges's. Since that script was twenty pages long and the final version of the autobiography came to sixty-five pages, this amounts to a whole Amazon River of commas. All this has been, to borrow words from Paul Theroux, 'the inevitable revisionism of the new wife'; but her attack on me detracts from Borges's essentially noble character and pre-empts serious discussion.

What I find puzzling today, nearly thirty years after the autobiography was written, is its neglect by serious Argentine scholars and its absence from any collected edition of its author's works. Also remarkable is the misinformation and misunderstanding that have continued to dog the piece. One critic and biographer claimed that it was conceived and written for an Argentine public. Another judged it to be an interview. The buffoon from the Spanish Royal Academy tells us it was the 'foreword to an American edition, of hundreds of thousands of copies, of *The Aleph and Other Stories*'. (He is wrong here on all counts.) Notes in *Textos recobrados 1919–1929*, a recent Argentine compilation, with scholarly pretensions, of early Borges writing, give further uninformed – and conflicting – remarks about the essay. Mentioning that it has been translated into several languages, the notes go on to state that its publication in Spanish was absolutely opposed by Borges. But apparently not quite so absolutely after all, since one sentence later we are told that Borges agreed to allow a version of his personal history to be published, in 1974, on the occasion of his seventy-fifth birthday, in the now defunct Buenos Aires newspaper *La Opinión*.

Despite Borges's reservations about the autobiography – neither explained nor speculated on in the *Textos recobrados* – it is nonetheless cited as a primary source of biographical information and quoted at length throughout the volume. As for Spanish translations, *Textos recobrados* lists a 1971 version by the prominent Mexican poet José Emilio Pacheco; in fact, what Pacheco translated was an excerpt of only a few pages. As for the translation in *La Opinión*, no mention is made – for presumably it was never examined – that it is incomplete or that its omissions were made for the reason that in 1974 Argentina's political climate was such that Borges's elegantly expressed anti-Peronist sentiments were felt to be in need of censorship and suppression. So, too, were his remarks on Old Norse metaphors. Apparently these were deemed too deep or abstruse for the Argentine reader. The translation itself – which was unsigned – is a travesty of Borges's impeccable style.

Amen.

On Translating Borges

Far away and long ago – that is to say, in November 1967, and in Harvard Square, in Cambridge, Massachusetts – I walked into Schoenhof's Foreign Bookshop and asked for a copy of Borges's collected poems. When the clerk brought me the book, he said, 'You know Borges is speaking here next week.' That was the first link in an invisible chain of cause and effect that brought Borges and me together in a working association that lasted for nearly five years. It was also the first link in a network that was soon to connect me with Buenos Aires in particular, with the River Plate in general, and with many dozens of friends the world over.

'Borges is speaking here next week.' The reverberation of the clerk's words seems never to have ended. Thirty years later, I was to receive from Bangladesh two copies of a small book. The volume, *Mexican Thoughts*, an anthology of prose pieces in translation, edited by one Razu Alauddin, is dedicated to me, both in Bengali and English. In an accompanying letter, my generous benefactor informed me that the book was a thank you for my work with Borges.

That any of this could have happened is a tribute to Borges and his international appeal.

I went home from Schoenhof's that day with a copy of Borges's *Obra poética* under my arm, and the following week I attended his public lecture in Memorial Hall. But the whole time, while I was reading the poems and listening to Borges and afterwards reading and studying the poetry further, I was transported to another realm. The words in the book and those spoken by the man on the stage were unmistakably one and the same, and I was struck by the gentle quality and humanity that each radiated. I had first come across it in lines of verse that Borges had written about his friend Elvira de Alvear, a Buenos Aires society woman whose life ended in madness. The poem, in the form of a bronze plaque, now adorns Elvira's tomb in the Recoleta cemetery.

She once had everything but one by one
Each thing abandoned her. We saw her armed
With beauty. The morning and the hard light
Of noon from their pinnacle revealed to her
The glorious kingdoms of the world. Evening
Wiped them away....

During the autumn of 1967 and winter of 1968, all of Cambridge was buzzing about Borges's presence. But I was probably the only one who went home after that November lecture and wrote Borges a letter.

In it, I asked if I could work with him on a volume of his poems in English translation. I told him that, a few years before, I had edited a selection of poems by Jorge Guillén, the Spanish poet who had lived and taught for years around Boston, and that my plan for Borges's poems was to produce something along similar lines. At this point, the hand of fate came heavily to intervene. Borges was notorious for never answering letters, and yet he answered mine, telling me to phone and to come and see him. I phoned. He asked me to come that very afternoon and to bring the poems I had done. 'I haven't done any poems yet,' I said in panic. 'Come anyway,' he said. That was the third of December. I knocked at Borges's door, walked in, and was to stay for nearly five years.

On that first afternoon, we talked about a recent poem of his that I liked very much. It was on an Anglo-Saxon figure, Hengist Cyning, who founded the first Saxon kingdom in what is now England. The poem is in two parts – the first, his epitaph, as it might have been carved in stone; the second, the king's own words as Borges made them up in the form of a dramatic monologue.

HENGIST CYNING

THE KING'S EPITAPH
Beneath this stone lies the body of Hengist
Who founded in these islands the first kingdom

Of the royal house of Odin
And glutted the screaming eagle's greed.

THE KING SPEAKS
I know not what runes will be scraped on the stone
But my words are these:
Beneath the heavens I was Hengist the mercenary.
My might and my courage I marketed to kings
Whose lands lay west over the water
Here at the edge of the sea
Called the Spear-Warrior;
But a man's might and his courage can
Not long bear being sold,
And so after cutting down all through the North
The foes of the Briton king,
From him too I took light and life together.
I like this kingdom that I seized with my sword;
It has rivers for the net and the oar
And long seasons of sun
And soil for the plough and for husbandry
And Britons for working the farms
And cities of stone which we shall allow
To crumble to ruin,
Because there dwell the ghosts of the dead.
But behind my back I know
These Britons brand me traitor,
Yet I have been true to my deeds and my daring
And to other men's care never yielded my destiny
And no one dared ever betray me.

The translation is one I made later, born of that first meeting. The extraordinary thing about that encounter, as I look back on it, was the fact of a poem about a Saxon king from the fifth century AD linking an older Argentine writer and a younger American, in Massachusetts, with the pair of us speaking in a flow of Spanish and English. The link, of course, was poetry and the music of words. I found out at the same time that Borges considered Guillén to be the finest poet then writing in the Spanish language. I also found out that Guillén's daughter, who was an old friend of mine, was accompanying Borges to a class he gave three times a week on contemporary Argentine writers. So when I had written my letter invoking Guillén's poems and his name, I could not have given myself a better recommendation.

Within a month, Borges and I had planned the whole book. Together we made a choice of one hundred poems, I began to commission poet-translators to make the English versions, we secured the necessary rights from the Argentine publisher, and I sold the project to an American publisher. Our method was to make a literal rough draft of each piece that was to be in the selection, which I would use both to help the translators get started and later to criticize their drafts as they came in. Sometimes letters would pass back and forth several times between me and a particular poet before each of us was satisfied with the result. Only after that would I take the poem to Borges for a final reading. Nearly a dozen American and British poets participated, and Borges and I were gratified by the way such distinguished writers flocked to the project. The eventual volume, Borges's *Selected Poems 1923–1967*, miraculously got off the ground in one month, but it was three years' work before a complete typescript was in hand, and production took still another year.

The winter of 1968 was an important time for Borges. Five of his books were then available in English (the first two had appeared in 1962); he was at Harvard, as the prestigious Charles Eliot Norton Professor of Poetry, to give six public lectures; and interest in his work in the United States was swelling to a crest. Through the poets involved in the *Selected Poems*, word got out about what Borges and I were up to in our meetings. In the beginning, these took place two or three times a week; soon they increased, and I was forced to move near Cambridge so that we could work in daily sessions. Borges would exhort me in his typically self-effacing way, 'When you write to the translators, tell them that in spite of my poems the translations must be good.' Of course, that was just the sort of remark that made our collaborators redouble their efforts. Borges and I began to be asked to organize readings, using our new translations, at a number of Greater Boston universities; and, a few months later – with several of the translators reading – at the YM-YWHA, in New York, the leading American poetry forum of the day.

Meanwhile, quite by chance, an unusual piece of information came my way. At the time we were working, Borges became the subject of a long interview, with several pages of photographs, in *Life en español*. The woman conducting it, Rita Guibert, was a frequent visitor at Borges's flat. One day I heard her ask him whether he had ever worked with any of his other translators the way he was working with me. No, never, he said. I found his reply remarkable. The several editors and translators involved in every one of those first five books of Borges's had, at one time or another, been in contact with him, but none had ever consulted him about his or her translation. It was a wonder to me that so many had overlooked anything so obvious. Borges was the easiest of men to approach, he was unfailingly co-operative, and he also spoke very fine English. The greatest resource of all – the author himself, steeped in the English language and its literature – had gone untapped. Moreover, I came to find, Borges's English was better than that of his translations. Later on, he confessed to me that one translator had contacted him a few years before to say she could find no equivalent in English for the title of his prose piece called 'El hacedor'. 'That was odd,' Borges said, 'because I thought up the title in English. It comes from the Scottish poet Dunbar. My Spanish title was a translation from the

English right from the start.' That title, of course, was 'The Maker'.

During this same period, I approached Borges about translating one of his short stories. We had been working on the poems for a couple of months by then, and I was curious to see whether we could apply the method we had evolved with the poetry to a longer work in prose. I warned him that I did not know enough about the Argentine to translate any of his stories on my own, so would only try my hand at it if he would help. I said we could then credit the finished product as having been translated in collaboration with the author. Borges was stunned by the suggestion. 'Of course, I'll help,' he said, 'but won't it hurt you to say that I took part?' I told him it would give the work more authority. 'Yes, I see that,' Borges said, 'but in my country a translator would be far too jealous to share credit with the author.'

The first story we translated together – it was 'The Other Death' – turned into one of the happiest and most fortuitous experiences of my life. Altogether I worked on the tale for about a week, including the three afternoon sessions that I spent on it with Borges. When we finished, I saw that what we had achieved was truer to the original tone and meaning and complex intentions of the author than any other translation of his into English until then. For his part, some time later, Borges told a class at Columbia University that

When we attempt a translation, or re-creation, of my poems or prose in English, we don't think of ourselves as being two men. We think we are really one mind at work.

At the outset of taking on 'The Other Death', on my own I had puzzled out and made a rough draft of the story. Since there were a number of elements in it so local that only an Argentine would understand them, and only an Argentine who spoke perfect English could have explained them, it was plain that I should not try to make perfect sentences in English of what I did not fully grasp. So I left gaps. I want to emphasize that my intention at this stage had been only to produce a makeshift draft that I could later go over with the author so as to get the meaning straight. Naturally, where simple sentences flowed out into solid English prose, I let them flow. When I completed my draft, I took it round to Borges. I read to him half a sentence or so in Spanish, followed by the equivalent portion of my rough-and-ready English version. Where the gaps fell, Borges would interrupt before I could explain my difficulty and he would say, 'Now in this next bit you won't understand such-and-such', and he would launch into an elaborate description of River Plate rural life or history that would provide me with exactly what I lacked. It soon became clear that the affinities between the plains of Argentina and those of the United States, with their vast open stretches of range land for grazing cattle, were greater than one at first imagined. There had to be terms common to both countries to express the similarity of their frontier histories. And there were – if only one avoided the dictionary, whose word-for-word equivalents are often of little value.

We forged ahead, sentence by sentence, sometimes feeling that what I had was good enough as it stood, sometimes revising extensively. On occasion, Borges corrected me; on occasion, I asked him to clarify. Often, no sooner had I read out one of my sentences than I saw ways of improving it before he could make the suggestion himself. In some cases, we offered an alternative or variations that I would return home with to test on my own. We would keep trying to free the sentences of cumbersome or indirect locutions. Passive constructions might become active; negative, positive. A phrase like '*marchaban desde el Sur*' – marched from the south – might become 'on their march north'. Our aim at this point was simply to get all of the Spanish into some kind of English, and in order to do so I needed a full understanding not only of the text but also of Borges's intentions. It did not matter to us yet that during the completion of this stage we might still be fairly literal or provisional. Often, in fact, we remained deliberately undecided about such details as finding the right word or phrase or shade of meaning.

After a session with Borges, I would return home and type out what we had gone over together, then set to work shaping and polishing the sentences and paragraphs, this time trying to supply the exact words. Now I would refer back to the Spanish only for checking rhythms and emphases. The concern would be with matters of tone and tension and style. To anyone who constructs a piece of prose and cares about style, this amounts to a slow and painstaking search for meanings to fit the sound patterns one keeps turning and turning in one's head. (Since good prose is written with the ear, music emerges before meaning.) After finishing this stage – and it was far and away the most time-consuming part of the job – I read the not-quite-final draft to Borges for approval and a last test. This time we completely ignored the Spanish and only tinkered here or there with a word.

I still remember how much trouble that complicated first sentence of 'The Other Death' gave me. It was the classic Borges opener, fulfilling his personal dictum that if you began with a long, involved sentence, by the time the reader got to the end of it he had made his way well into the story and would be hooked. I must have sat there for over an hour on that sentence alone, taking it apart and putting it together, testing it and re-testing it for crucial balances and rhythms. What made the sentence so hard was its multiple clauses. Here it is:

I have mislaid the letter, but a couple of years or so ago Gannon wrote to me from his ranch up in Gualeguaychú saying he would send me a translation, perhaps the very first into Spanish, of Ralph Waldo Emerson's poem 'The Past', and adding in a PS that don Pedro Damián, whom I might recall, had a few nights earlier died of a lung ailment.

I am quite fond of that sentence, not only because it was the first prose of Borges's that I ever translated but also because to me it stands for the beginning – the first story itself, the method we invented there on the spot, and, gratifyingly, the contract it landed us from the *New Yorker*. They invited us to submit to them any of Borges's work previously untranslated – stories, poems, and essays, past and to come. It was only years later that I learned from the magazine's then editor William Shawn that I was the only translator they ever had under contract.

The long sentence quoted above, I hasten to point out, is not the version of it that appeared in print either in the magazine or in the volume it was subsequently destined for, in 1970, *The Aleph and Other Stories*. On two occasions since then, in quoting the sentence I have revised it. I mention this to indicate that a translation, like any other piece of writing, can always be improved; and also to show that the work of the translator, like that of any other craftsman, gets better with experience.

Borges left Cambridge to return to Argentina in mid-April 1968, and several months later I joined him in Buenos Aires. In the interval, a New York publisher had found me and asked me to sort out the translation rights to Borges's work, which were hopelessly entangled and disputed among several American publishers. They also asked me to translate into English for them as many of Borges's books as I could lay my hands on. So keen (and innocent) was this publishing house that they told me to sign up every last one of Borges's still untranslated novels. When I let them in on the secret that the man had never written a novel they did not flinch. Whatever there was, I was instructed, get it. In the end, I was to see eleven of Borges's books into print in English, and even now, thirty or so years on, another small handful are still in progress.

After I went to live in Argentina, where I stayed for nearly four years, those bits of any text I did not understand and left blank in my early drafts got fewer and fewer. But nothing changed with regard to the tacit assumptions and agreements that underlay the method that Borges and I had worked out for ourselves. We agreed, for example, that a translation should not sound like a translation but should read as though it had been written directly in the language into which it was being made. While this may appear obvious, for a writer and translator as accomplished as Vladimir Nabokov the opposite held true. He maintained that a translation should sound like a translation. But Borges and I wanted his translations to read like original works. He once confessed to me that when earlier versions of his stories were read to him he recognized the particular piece as his but always thought he wrote better than that. In the preface to *The Aleph and Other Stories*, we stated:

Perhaps the chief justification of this book is the translation itself, which we have undertaken in what may be a new way. Working closely together in daily sessions, we have tried to make these stories read as though they had been written in English. We do not consider English and Spanish as compounded of sets of easily interchangeable synonyms; they are two quite different ways of looking at the world, each with a nature of its own. English, for example, is far more physical than Spanish. We have therefore shunned the dictionary as much as possible and done our best to rethink every sentence in English words. This venture does not necessarily mean that we have willfully tampered with the original, though in certain cases we have supplied the American reader with those things – geographical, topographical, and historical – taken for granted by any Argentine.

Were those words being written today, for 'American' I would have suggested 'English-speaking'.

Borges and I further agreed that in translating from Spanish into English, words with Anglo-Saxon roots are preferable to words of Latin origin. Often this means that the first word suggested by the Spanish should be avoided. For instance, for '*solitario*' one would translate not 'solitary' but 'lonely'; for '*rígido*', not 'rigid' but 'stiff'. On a number of occasions Borges said he could never understand why his early translators would translate '*habitación oscura*' into 'obscure habitation' when what he meant was 'dark room'. Of course, when choosing the first word suggested by the Spanish there is the danger of falling into the trap of the false cognate, or false association. The translation of one Borges story is badly marred at a crucial point when the word '*discutir*', 'to argue', is translated as 'to discuss'. A professor of Spanish-American literature at an American university once criticized me in print for having translated Borges's words '*más notorio atributo*' as 'most obvious trait'. He wanted the translation to read 'most notorious atribute', not only ignoring the context of the phrase but also being caught out by the false cognate. '*Notorio*' in this instance meant simply 'noteworthy', or 'obvious', without the negative connotation the word carries in English.

Borges has a marvellous prose poem about Shakespeare called 'Everything and Nothing'. In the opening line, Borges described Shakespeare's words as '*copiosas, fantásticas y agitadas*'. One translation of this reads, 'copious, fantastic, and agitated'; a second, 'copious, imaginative, and emotional'. This is distinctly better and shows that the translator is not just translating the words but is thinking about their meaning in terms of Shakespeare. A third translation reads,

'copious, fantastic, and stormy'. A fourth, 'multitudinous, and of a fantastical and agitated turn' – a solution both long-winded and stodgy. A fifth version
– the one made by Borges and me – reads, 'swarm-
ing, fanciful, and excited'.

There were other factors working for us that under-
pinned our method. Foremost was Borges's command
of English and his sense of English prose style. An
anecdote will illustrate just how sensitive he was to
English. In 1964, Borges fixed to his collected poems
the following paragraph, taken from one of Robert
Louis Stevenson's letters:

> I do not set up to be a poet. Only an all-round literary man:
> a man who talks, not one who sings.... Excuse this little apol-
> ogy; but I don't like to come before people who have a note of
> song and let it be supposed I do not know the difference.

As the Spanish-language editions of Borges's work
were riddled with errors, I thought I had better look
that quote up in Volume II, p. 77, of the edition
Borges had cited. When I did, sure enough, I found
an error – but not a printer's error. What I found was
that Borges had tampered with the text. It was not,
as in his version, 'Excuse this little apology; but I
don't like to come before people', etc. Rather, the
correct text ran: 'Excuse this little apology for my
house; but I don't like to come before people', and
so on. When I asked Borges why he had suppressed

the words 'for my house' he said it was because they sounded silly and thereby weakened the text. But he added that for our edition of his poetry I could print the epigraph any way I liked.

A few years later, in London, travelling with Borges – it is uncanny how this takes the shape of a Borges story – I bought the beautiful twenty-six-volume Vailima edition of Stevenson's works. Back in Buenos Aires, I don't know for what reason, I checked the source of the epigraph again; this edition had been published twenty-four years after the one Borges had used, and it had been newly edited as well. There I found that the quote read: 'Excuse this little apology for my muse ...' Muse, not house. Now it made perfect sense. The original letter had been handwritten, and its editor had misread the word 'muse' as 'house'. Borges, without having seen the original, had sensed the mistake. It is well known, of course, that Borges's feeling for English prose often amounted to a preference for the English language over his own as a writing medium.

Let me further illustrate our method of translation by applying it to a short prose text – that of the story 'Pedro Salvadores'.

Three pages long, 'Pedro Salvadores' is a tale set in Buenos Aires during the Rosas dictatorship some hundred and fifty years ago. To escape certain death at the hands of the authorities, a man goes into hiding and lives for nine years in the darkness of his own cellar. Borges wrote the story in June 1969, for his book *In Praise of Darkness*. He had carried the tale in his head for a long time, having first heard it from his mother, who in turn had heard it from her father. In the autumn of 1967, while at Harvard, Borges had dictated three sentences of it in English to his secretary, John Murchison, an Anglo-Argentine graduate student, to whom the story was later dedicated. The tale was then laid aside. Our problem in the translation was how to make the narrative's complex background in Argentine history wholly intelligible to the English-speaking reader.

At the outset, Borges tells us that one of the three characters in the story is the dictator's 'overpowering shadow', but, because every Argentine knows who that dictator was, he is not mentioned by name except obliquely at the story's close. Similarly, a battle is mentioned without our being told its significance. Again, Borges takes his reader's knowledge for granted, just as no American writer would have to spell out the significance of Yorktown or Appomattox, or an English writer Hastings or Waterloo. We learn in passing that Salvadores is a Unitarian; we learn that a group of nightriders are the *mazorca*; and there is a mysterious reference to 'blue chinaware'. None of the terms or words is explained. How were we going to handle these vital details in the English version? And then, to complicate matters still more, there was the fact that the story is so brief – it runs to no more than six or seven hundred words in the original – that any elucidation we intended to work into our English would have to be very deftly woven. What was at stake in the translation was the difference between reading two or three interesting pages, in which the reader would never quite know what was going on, and reading a story that could be both understood and felt.

'A man, a woman, and the overpowering shadow of a dictator are the three characters', the second paragraph begins. The man was named Pedro Salvadores; Borges's grandfather had seen him days or weeks after the battle of Caseros. At this point I asked Borges what the significance of the battle of Caseros was. 'It was Rosas' downfall,' Borges told me. I suggested that we say that, and he agreed. First problem solved. We wrote, 'My grandfather Acevedo saw him days or weeks after the dictator's downfall in the battle of Caseros.' The story continues: 'Pedro Salvadores may have been no different from anyone else, but the years and his fate set him apart. He was a gentleman like many other gentlemen of his day. He owned (let us suppose) a ranch in the country and....' Here we were in difficulty again. The Spanish at this point reads, '*y era unitario*' – 'and was a Unitarian'. Borges thought that this piece of Argentine history would be lost on the English-speaking reader and should therefore be left out. It seemed

to me, however, that if he supplied me with the
background we could make the reference meaningful in the translation. I also felt that it was essential
to the story that the two opposing sides be firmly
established, and what better place than here? Salvadores was a Unitarian; Rosas, a Federalist. But we
did not want to complicate matters by introducing
a new term. I asked Borges whether this meant that
Salvadores was opposed to the tyranny. The answer
was yes. Then that's what we'll say, I suggested, and
with the addition of four words we had a solution to
the Unitarian problem. Pleased and amused, Borges
ribbed me. 'Now you're quite sure', he said, 'that
when our readers see Unitarian they won't be thinking Emerson and New England?' At this juncture,
our translation ran, 'He owned (let us suppose) a
ranch in the country and, opposed to the tyranny,
was on the Unitarian side.'

It is here, in the sixth sentence of the paragraph,
that Borges mentions the second character, the
woman. We are told only that her family name was
Planes; then the sentence goes on to say that Salvadores and his wife '*vivían en la calle Suipacha, no
lejos de la esquina del Temple*' – 'lived in Suipacha
Street, not far from the corner of Temple'. Without
my asking, Borges quickly explained that Temple
did not exist any longer but was the old name for
Viamonte. 'But since these streets will mean nothing
to the reader, you can leave them out if you want

to,' he said. 'Or, instead, you might simply say "the heart of Buenos Aires".' I argued that in reading English writers – this was before I lived in England – though London streets meant little to me, I was grateful for their names all the same, since in my imagination they made London more real. Borges agreed that this was true, so we retained the names. But I liked his idea and thought we should use it as well; also, remembering what he had told me about the topography of old Buenos Aires – how, for example, the present Barrio Norte was once the edge of town – it occurred to me that if we worked in the one word 'now' we could hint at the spread of the city during the past century. We ended up with this: 'they lived together on Suipacha Street near the corner of Temple in what is now the heart of Buenos Aires.'

Next comes a description of their home, a typical Buenos Aires house of the day, 'with a street door, a long arched entranceway, inner grillwork gate' and '*la hondura de los patios*' – 'a depth of patios'. I was already familiar with this metaphor from one of Borges's poems that we had worked on in Cambridge and by this time, as I was living in Buenos Aires, I knew at first hand what a depth of patios meant. The old houses of Buenos Aires are narrow and extraordinarily deep, having a succession of patios, strung out one behind the other. The first of these might have black-and-white chessboard paving; the third, usually unpaved, a grapevine. We decided that the best way of expressing this in English was to say 'a row of two or three patios'. All these years later, however, I wonder whether 'a depth of patios' would not have been better.

At this point in the Spanish text, the background information concludes and the narrative begins. I felt that here was where we should say something about the dictator. Borges and I were in agreement that our readers should be told who he was. At the head of the paragraph we learned that the characters were three; then we were given something about each of the first two. This was the place, then, to round out the presentation of the characters and to mention Rosas. We simply added this short line to the story: 'The dictator, of course, was Rosas.' Then we began a new paragraph.

'One night around 1842,' the paragraph starts out, 'Salvadores and his wife heard the growing, muffled sound of horses' hooves out on the unpaved street and the riders shouting their drunken *vivas* and their threats.' Now comes the reference to the *mazorca*, which we would have to explain. After Borges had described them to me, it seemed that they were the storm troopers of that era. The most straightforward solution we could think of was to say, 'This time Rosas' henchmen did not ride on.' Three sentences later, the word is used again, but having just been explained, we felt that in this instance we could get

away without translating or otherwise explaining it.
The story continues:

After the shouts came repeated knocks at the door; while the
men began forcing it, Salvadores was able to pull the dining-
room table aside, lift the rug, and hide himself down in the
cellar. His wife dragged the table back in place. The *mazorca*
broke into the house; they had come to take Salvadores. The
woman said her husband had run away to Montevideo. The men
did not believe her; they flogged her, they smashed all the blue
chinaware....

Here, with the mention of blue chinaware, was
our last problem, but it was only by chance that I
found this out. Somehow, when I first read Borges's
Spanish, '*rompieron toda la vajilla celeste*', my curiosity was roused. Did he mean that they smashed *all*
Salvadores's china, which happened to be blue, or
was it that among all the crockery they smashed only
the blue pieces? Only the blue, Borges informed me,
because blue was the Unitarian colour. And when
the Argentine reader sees '*vajilla celeste*', I wanted to
know, does he understand at once what you are talking about? Yes, Borges said, everyone knew. In that
case, we had to see to it that every reader in English
knew too. The best way to do this, I thought, was to
introduce the information as a parenthesis enclosed
by brackets. It was a usage Borges often employed.
I wrote into the draft, '(for blue was the colour of the

Unitarians)'; but as soon as the words were on the page I saw how three of them could be cut. We ended up with this: 'The men did not believe her; they flogged her, they smashed all the blue china-ware (blue was the Unitarian colour), they searched the whole house, but they never thought of lifting the rug.' From here on, the rest of 'Pedro Salvadores' was fairly easy going. Our whole work together on the translation had taken place in two short sessions. Curiously, 'Pedro Salvadores' appeared in print in English translation in the *New York Review of Books* even before it appeared in Spanish.

On a number of occasions, Borges and I were able to make and publish new translations of some of his finest tales – ones translated into English even three or more times previously. I have likened our achieve-ment in these stories to the cleaning of old pictures. In our effort, we tried hard to restore the clarity, the sharpness, and the colour of the originals. Once, when I read him the finished draft of his celebrated story 'The Circular Ruins', Borges wept. '*Caramba*,' he said, 'I wish I could still write like that.' These were the versions of his work that Borges had long awaited and that he now considered to be definitive.

A Translator's Guide

No criticism can be instructive which descends not to particulars, and is not full of examples and illustrations.
– David Hume, *Of Simplicity and Refinement in Writing*

Translation, literary translation, is a branch of writing. If writing is an art, translation is an art; if writing is a craft, translation is a craft. After thirty years of practice in this branch of writing, I find 'craft' the better term. Perhaps it is a matter of taste. 'Art' has too grand a ring to it.

Borges once remarked that 'The translator is a very close reader; there is not much difference between translating and reading.' Simple and succinct. Most talk about translation, alas, takes place on a dizzyingly rarefied plane. 'The hermeneutic motion, the act of elicitation and appropriative transfer of meaning, is fourfold,' writes one exegete, who himself stands in need of translation. Like Borges, I prefer to keep it simple. Translation, in my workaday life, amounts to saying it in English. Is this English? is the question I put to myself a hundred times a week.

Are the following lines English? 'Streaks of moonlight filtered through the curtain's lace toward the satin pillow, which soaked them up. The hand of the new bride, beside her dark hair, offered its palm up defensively.... Then the palm suddenly clenched, not so the perfect face, which remained relaxed, made up in cosmetics from rose to blue.' The answer is no; they are pure pidgin – yet they were published by one of New York's most prestigious houses.

So, for the benefit of the slack editor of this illiterate muddle (as well as for any other editor or aspirant), here is my instant training course. Which of the following is the best translation? Or, in my terms, which is the best English?

'The torrential rains, Captain Liddell Hart comments, caused this delay, an insignificant one, to be sure.'

'He comments that torrential rain caused this delay – which lacked any special significance.'

'Torrential rains (notes Capt. Liddell Hart) were the cause of that delay – a delay that entailed no great consequences, as it turns out.'

'The cause of this otherwise inconsequential delay, he goes on, was torrential rain.'

The first three will be found in the published versions of one of Borges's most famous stories. The fourth is my own.

The third example, in its wordiness, in its repetition of 'delay' and 'that', is awkward and reveals the translator's inability to cope with a sentence that contains several clauses. The first 'that', a demonstrative pronoun, would have made for a sharper reading had it been translated as 'this'. The word 'entailed' here is incorrectly used; also incorrect is the tense of 'turns', which should have been 'turned'. There is in addition something spurious about the word order. The tip-off is the limp 'as it turns out', which closes the sentence with a whimper.

The first example would have gained in concision had 'The torrential rains' been pruned to 'Torrential rain'. Again, the close is limp. The second example fails on two counts. It does not make clear exactly what lacks special significance, and – in common with the previous examples – the words at the end simply dangle. The fourth version is clear and concise. The structure of the sentence, its word order, is natural to effective English.

It is easier when you have two or more versions in front of you, but what, asks the editor, do I do when faced with something like this: 'I don't know who was the victim of who, in that house of sugar, which now stands empty.' He could start by asking himself whether this is good English. The answer is no, because it fails to observe the natural order of an effective English sentence, which follows the pattern 2-3-1, with the second most important element coming first, the least important lying in the middle, and the most important, like a punch line, coming at the end. Remaining oblivious of the original Spanish and merely reworking the above, we should get this: 'In that house of sugar, which now stands empty, I don't know who was the victim of whom.'

Following these guidelines, let's look at some good and bad examples of the craft.

Good: 'He's manic about his style and, to his publisher's despair, pitiless about last-minute tinkering.'

Good: 'My own repeated forays up and down the carriages in search of other passengers, or at least of a guard who might want to see my ticket, were also fruitless.'

Good: 'I put two more shot on the line and closed them with my teeth. Then I put a fresh salmon egg on and cast out where the water dropped over a shelf into the pool.'

The above examples are spare, natural, and sound like English. The third is English – Raymond Carver's. One should not be able to tell the difference.

Bad: 'Those who don't see each other often don't know what to say.' This is limp and unmusical as well as unclear. The Spanish it is trying to render is: *Todas las personas que no se ven a menudo, no saben qué decirse.* I would venture this: 'People who seldom meet have little to talk about when they do.' The three words at the end are not in the Spanish, but English sense demands them. The translator of Latin American writing has to be something of an editor as well, it must be remembered, since Latin American publishers rarely work their authors as hard as we work ours.

Bad. 'Menard ... has enriched, by means of a new technique, the halting and rudimentary art of reading: this new technique is one of deliberate anachronism and the erroneous attribution.'

Bad. 'Menard ... has enriched, by means of a new technique, the hesitant and rudimentary art of reading: the technique is one of deliberate anachronism and erroneous attributions.'

Bad. 'Menard has ... enriched the slow and rudimentary art of reading by means of a new technique – the technique of deliberate anachronism and fallacious attribution.'

Good. 'Through a new technique, using deliberate anachronisms and false attributions, Menard ... has enriched the static, fledgling art of reading.'

All four of these, again, are from Borges. The first three examples are wordy and repetitive. 'By means of' is translatorese. 'Hesitant' (or 'halting' or 'slow') and 'rudimentary' fail to illuminate the noun phrase they modify. The translators, rather than thinking, were lazily settling for the first words suggested by the Spanish. The very crux of the sentence, the reference to the 'art' of reading – which happens also to be the climax of the story – has been buried away and remains opaque. In these examples, the translators linked the two adjectives that modify 'art' with the word 'and', oblivious of the fact that – unlike Spanish – adjectives in English are commonly separated by a comma. Finally, the word order: in the first three, the sentence flounders, the punch is lost. These three form part of the Borges canon; the fourth has so far not appeared in any collection of his work.

Four more from the same story, leading this time with the Spanish:

Dedicó sus escrúpulos y vigilias a repetir en un idioma ajeno un libro preexistente.

'He dedicated his conscience and nightly studies to the repetition of a pre-existing book in a foreign tongue.'

'He dedicated his scruples and his sleepless nights to repeating an already extant book in an alien tongue.'

'He dedicated his scruples and his nights "lit by midnight oil" to repeating in a foreign tongue a book that already existed.'

'He devoted his utmost care and attention to reproducing, in a language not his own, a book that already existed.'

Literalness, word-for-word slavishness, is the bugbear of translation. We want the right words in the right order; we want rhythm and tone. We want a great deal of common sense. And then we want what the late Humberto Costantini used to call '*ese polvo de oro*' – that sprinkle of gold dust. In other words, the final touch that makes everything fit together and spring alive. Ezra Pound once found it necessary to preach that poetry should be as well written as prose. It ought to be axiomatic in the publishing world today, but it is not, that a translation should be as well written (and rewritten) as any other piece of writing.

At the risk of complicating matters (but to give the other side its due), I must point out that no less eminent a stylist than Nabokov felt otherwise about translation. He held that a translation should read like a translation. And he must have had a great following, because to my ear most translation today – especially the translation of Latin-American writers – holds to the Nabokovian line. Maybe this explains why Nabokov's own writing always sounded like translation to me. I do not dispute his genius, but his written English was not that of a native speaker.

A good translation, like good vodka, should leave you breathless in at least two of the word's many senses. Aspiring to inconspicuousness, invisibility, it should bear no telltale trace of the original. A translation should also be bracing. Since it will have all the qualities of good native work, a good translation into English should – I cannot express it more simply – read like English.

Backward Glances

In the ten years since his death, Jorge Luis Borges – the favourite of other writers round the world, the darling of academics everywhere – has continued to command a discerning small readership for his revolutionary short stories. Except in his own country, Argentina, where he is widely bought (because of his fame abroad), little read, and greatly misunderstood.

Now we enter a new phase in the Borges phenomenon. So celebrated was he at the time he died that the audience for his life story threatened to overtake the audience for his books. Now it has. James Woodall's is the third biography of Borges to have come across my table in the past few months. And Borges's widow, according to Woodall, trumpets the fact that we stand to be treated to a dozen or so more. Grotesque. Especially for a man who thought of himself first and foremost as a reader.

Did Borges live a life worth a single full-blown treatment, let alone fifteen? A quarter of a century ago, he and I sat down to write up his personal history, in English, and we managed it in fewer than sixty pages. It was a simple tale designed as a much-needed framework for the stories and poems that were puzzling and intriguing readers throughout the English-speaking world. Myopic and frail as a boy, Borges was only too aware in later years that he was no Hemingway. In the modest 1970 memoir, he said so: 'As most of my people had been soldiers ... and I knew I would never be, I felt ashamed, quite early, to be a bookish kind of person and not a man of action.'

Soon after the essay appeared, Borges had qualms about it. For his taste, it held too much factual information, too many dates. He himself had written the life of a minor Buenos Aires poet, Evaristo Carriego, back in 1930. Astonishingly, the book contained but six dates. A chronological account of Carriego's life, Borges held, was inappropriate. 'Only a timeless description ... can bring him back to us.' It was the patterns in the poet's life, his essence, his eternity, that interested Borges. As biographer, he saw his role as one of making us *become* Carriego, 'not of mirroring him'. Despite the acclaim his autobiography was given when it first appeared in the *New Yorker* magazine, Borges told me that he saw his life more in terms of Coleridge's *Biographia Literaria* – in other words, as a discussion of his thought and reading.

Sensibly, Woodall has opted for chronology and documentation, not for mirroring Borges. But unfortunately, except for his final fifteen or so years – long after his best work was behind him – Borges lived a dullish sort of life. Then, when dizzying fame held him in its grip, the life turned into a sordid circus. Publishers competed for his hack work, while universities and governments competed to heap honours on him. He never refused the latter, since the travel this entailed was his only chance to be close to the much younger woman he was to marry on his death-bed.

Later, widow, family, and housemaid competed for his money and possessions. Seven months before his end, wife-to-be whisked him off to die in Geneva, the scene of his schooldays, and lied about his illness, got his will changed, married him, buried him, then started up a foundation in his name in Buenos Aires, where she now signs his books at the annual local book fair and refuses to honour his commitments.

Woodall, who makes his book come alive with the parallel story of his two trips to Buenos Aires on the track of the life, nibbles away at the fringes of this frenzied drama but fails to follow up the leads and do it justice. A pity, for it would have made a better story than the early years of quiet friendships and omnivorous reading and national history that, despite Woodall's care and pains, are too dull and too local for the general English-speaking reader. Oddly, I found Woodall better, sharper, more succinct, when he was judging Borges's achievements and defining his essence than when he mirrored his days.

In the end, perhaps Borges was right, and the real book of his life – the one of his mind – is yet to be written. In it, I would like to see the man distinguished from his work. To view Borges whole it would be good to glimpse the weaker side of his character. So far no biographer has attempted this. The Borges I worked with and whose vicissitudes I shared for several years was a lovable, generous maverick. But at the same time he was often disloyal, bigoted, thoughtless, irresponsible, and politically frivolous. He was a fair representative of a certain class of Argentine, the patrician come down in life. He was civilized, spoiled, curious, the perfect amateur with a touch of genius about him.

[1996]

BORGES REMEMBERED

The Borges I knew and worked with – the one still fresh in my memory these twenty years since his death, the one I search for in his myriad biographies and cannot find – the everyday Borges, existed in a rarefied atmosphere. Protected and spoiled by his family, he never had to seek a job until he was close to forty. He always lived at home, and even at seventy-one, when he walked out on a disastrous marriage, he went back to his mother. Borges's inner life was lived in books, in philosophical quandaries, in thinking. He adored women but had no sexual success with them. Nor was he a practical man. Once, in Salt Lake City, as we sat side by side in barber chairs having our hair cut, an attendant approached and asked if I wanted my shoes shined. I nodded a yes for myself and for Borges, who suddenly flared. He didn't want anyone polishing his shoes, claiming that he never did them at home. No, I pointed out to him, his maid Fani always polished them for him.

Borges courted controversy, often heedlessly, sometimes to the point of foolhardiness. Whatever made him accept a medal from Pinochet I will never fathom. It cost him the Nobel Prize. He was little interested in politics or world affairs yet would make ill-informed statements on issues he knew nothing about. Once, at Harvard, in an interview with a young journalist, he praised the war in Vietnam, which at the moment all of America was repudiating; another time he emerged from a meeting with Jorge Videla, one of the architects of Argentina's dirty war, and pronounced that the new government – a military takeover – was in the hands of gentlemen. But to give him his due, Borges had also been a staunch anti-Nazi and defender of the Jews when in Buenos Aires such a stand was unfashionable. His blindness isolated him, and he sometimes used this as an excuse. At home he was surrounded and swayed by members of his own class, the old oligarchy, reactionary dinosaurs who lived in an imaginary past. Borges once refused to accede to Neruda's request for a meeting, despite his mother's and my pleas to the contrary. Neruda, as a Communist, was a leper. It was not that Borges had no sympathy for the downtrodden and dispossessed. He simply did not know they existed.

But one could not help admiring him for his modest existence, for the fact that outside of a few books he had no interest in material things. He would eat a little boiled rice, sometimes with an egg on it. On winter evenings, returning from work, he liked a cup of steaming chocolate. Shamefaced about having accepted membership in the stodgy Argentine Academy of Letters, he fell back on a claim that they served the best hot chocolate in town. He was shy about his false teeth, which he used to rinse after a meal, telling me not to look. We often stood side by side at urinals, and he would ask me to read aloud any dirty graffiti that adorned the walls. The more graphic they were, the more he enjoyed them, for he was no prude. He rarely listened to music, finding it too emotional. He seldom showed feelings and, despite his many adversities, never wallowed in self-pity, proclaiming we had a duty to happiness. For him there were no sacred cows; he made fun of everything and everybody. He chided me with the sobriquet Napoléon whenever I tried to hurry him to appointments. To brush off importuning individuals, he would agree to things he had no intention of doing – writing an article for an encyclopedia, say, or meeting a top political figure. He admired the ethics, the civic-mindedness, of the Anglo-Saxon, but he himself often lapsed into the South American usage he claimed to despise. Nor was he above telling what he considered white lies in order to explain away actions that later came to embarrass him.

We remained friends – and he confided in me – to the end, yet stories still circulate about our having fallen out, about his having thrown me out of his house. Alas, being close to Borges came with a price, in my case laying me open to the smouldering envy of petty academics and erstwhile friends, gossipmongers who never knew the real man but to whom, on his pedestal, Borges was a god.

[2006]

THE OTHER BORGES

Only a few weeks ago, I caught a programme on BBC Radio 4 in which Borges's recorded voice told the world that when he and I sat down to translate his stories and poems we did not regard what we were doing as work but rather as fun. That must have been in 1970 or 1971. And he was right. Our work together was fun; he made it so. There was nothing stodgy about Borges, nothing formidable or forbidding. He knew his work was a cosmic game and he never wanted to be seen taking it or himself too seriously.

That, of course, was the public persona, and while it was perfectly true it was far from the whole story. Behind this man was the buttoned-up Borges no one ever glimpsed, the Borges he never allowed anyone to glimpse. But you do not work with a man day in and day out for years, in his native city, in his home, befriended by his family and his closest friends, often travelling with him on journeys halfway round the world, without getting to see behind the protective wall that – in Borges's case – he has erected round himself and that keeps the private man in stultifying isolation.

Borges's cocoon was a complicated affair, made up, in part, of his ancestry, which imbued him with English reserve and undemonstrativeness and with what I can only surmise was a fear of displaying emotion. But another part of it can be attributed to his studies in Indian philosophy, Hindu and Buddhist, certain precepts of which he adopted in order to seal off his demons. One of those demons was self-disgust with an ageing and decaying body. Another was the fact of the mortifying failure he experienced in his sexual relations with women, which of course resulted in total suppression. What Borges made himself believe was that the world is an illusion.

Looking back now – not on the work but on the private experiences that circumstances forced me to share with Borges – I see a desperately lonely and desperately sad man. The late marriage to Elsa was a demeaning experience, and its break-up utterly humiliating. One day, shortly after his separation, Borges asked me to accompany him to the bank to check how much money was in their joint account. I stood beside him at the teller's window as the clerk reported that there was none. So stricken was Borges by the news that he began to slip to the floor, and I had to prop him up. Then, all the way back to his flat, he kept repeating that it could not be, that there had to be some mistake. It turned out that as soon as we left the bank that day, the teller phoned Elsa to report that Borges had been there making inquiries. Full of glee, the vengeful wife threw it in his face that he had not been able to locate the money. In fact, she had transferred it to a new account in the same bank in her sole name.

We made our getaway out of Buenos Aires on the morning his lawyers and a crew of removal men went around to the marital flat to retrieve the only possessions that mattered to him – his books. Hidden away in another town, we had to buy Borges some new clothes, a suit, a pair of pyjamas. When we'd done so, the clerk asked me what we wanted to do with Borges's old suit. I told him to wrap it up and we'd take it with us. Without a word he held the trousers up to the light and wiggled his finger in a hole in the seat that was the size of a two-pound coin. This was the way Elsa sent the poor man out into the street to his job at the National Library. Yet had he known he would not have lowered himself to grumble or complain. And this defencelessness, this trait of humility and resignation in him, I found cruelly sad.

Sometimes the responsibility he placed on me was unnerving. In London, in 1971, during a fortnight's stay in the maze and warren of Brown's Hotel, Borges asked me to lock him into his room at night and take the key away with me. Before I left him I would lay out his next day's clothes at the foot of his bed, and the following morning, on entering his room, draw his bath for him. There was something touching and childlike about his trust.

He never asked me to do anything for him except occasionally to read him a story by Kipling or Stevenson. Whatever needed doing – a letter answered, someone spoken to on his behalf to get him out of something he did not want to do or into something he did want – I volunteered. There was an unworldliness about him that was not calculated. I remember in his final years when we were at work together on some of his last poems, the moment I entered his flat he would ask straightaway if I were free for dinner that evening. I invariably was. But I could see at once, with the question settled, that he would relax and enjoy the task ahead, because the problem of a yawning, empty night alone had been resolved.

As I look back now, twenty-three years after his death, I see – or think I see – that to Borges the poet and story-teller I was both a colleague and a collaborator. But to the other Borges, who in my memories sits alone in arid darkness waiting for someone to come, I was a friend.

[2009]

Afterword

The essay 'In Memory of Borges', written in 1987 – the year after Borges's death – was commissioned by Robin Baird-Smith and originally appeared as an introduction to a volume of the same name (Constable, 1988), which collected the first series of the Anglo-Argentine Society of London's annual Jorge Luis Borges lecture. The piece appeared again, translated into Italian by Raul Montanari, in *In quante lingue si può sognare?* (Leonardo Editore, 1991), a small volume that included lectures by Borges, Graham Greene, and Mario Vargas Llosa.

'Borges and His Interpreters' grew out of a talk commissioned by Judith Bumpus, in 1977, for Radio 3.

'Evaristo Carriego: Borges as Biographer' was first written to introduce Borges's book on the poet Evaristo Carriego when the volume was published in an English translation by Dutton, in New York, in 1984. The piece had previously appeared, in extended form, in the *Bennington Review*. The present version incorporates much new material.

'Borges and His Autobiography' was planned as a foreword to the Argentine edition of Borges's

'Autobiographical Essay', which was published in book form, in a Spanish translation, in April 1999. In the end, the book's pusillanimous Buenos Aires publisher failed to use the piece. Subsequently enlarged and updated, the essay is meant to serve as the introduction to a future English edition of Borges's life history. A slightly shorter version of the present text, titled 'The good reader', has been printed in *The Times Literary Supplement*.

Part of 'On Translating Borges' was cannibalized from a talk given in 1969 at the University of Oklahoma and later published in the *Antioch Review*, in *Books Abroad*, and after that in *The Cardinal Points of Borges*, edited by Lowell Dunham and Ivar Ivask (University of Oklahoma Press, 1971). Elements of an earlier piece about working with Borges, published in *Encounter*, have also found their way into the present essay. Most of the text printed here appeared in *The Times Literary Supplement*. I am grateful to Alan Jenkins, Deputy Editor of the *TLS*, for having wormed the piece out of me and for his many valuable suggestions. A translation into Spanish by Marcial Souto, titled 'Traducir a Borges', has appeared in the *Revista de Occidente*.

'A Translator's Guide' was first printed, under another title, in the *Independent*. It was reprinted in the booklet *Primer Encuentro de Editores*, published in Buenos Aires, in 1989, by the Consejo Argentino para las Relaciones Internacionales for a conference of editors, translators, and literary agents organized by the Argentine writer Alejandro Manara. Very much in the tenor in which this little credo was conceived, and especially in its advocacy of rewriting, it has been modified for each new appearance.

'A Footnote to Infamy' was commissioned by Ronald Christ and printed (in a different form) in *Review 73*, a publication of the Center for Inter-American Relations, in New York, as part of a special feature to mark the first English translation of Borges's *A Universal History of Infamy*. The main sections of the piece were written in a light-hearted vein.

The two remaining essays, 'Borges at Play' and 'Borges and His Sources', had their origin in talks and lectures delivered over the years at schools and universities in England, Scotland, Argentina, the United States, Canada, and Australia. It goes without saying that in the cases of these addresses they have been pruned, readjusted, and rewritten for their appearance here.

I am indebted to my friend Francis Spencer, poet, teacher, and reader, who studied various drafts of the typescript and gave me a good deal of advice and direction. At certain points, in areas of his own interest and expertise, he assisted me in making connections and also sent me back to delve deeper. I wish additionally to thank Marcial Souto, my Barcelona colleague, for his hand in dreaming up the volume and for his unstinting encouragement and practical assistance in its development. Thanks are also due to my two mainstays, Susan Ashe and Warwick Collins, for their criticism and suggestions, and to Melissa Balfour for help in the essay on Borges's autobiography. Jean and Neil Merritt kindly read the final script and pointed out a number of lapses, now gratefully corrected, that arose mainly from my old roots in American English. The typescript benefited too from the critical eye of René de Costa, who once invited me to contribute to a conference on Borges's early work at the University of Chicago.

Repeating the advice of his friend Alfonso Reyes, the Mexican writer and diplomat, Borges suggested that one way of ridding yourself of what you have written is to publish it. I note that some of my work here goes back forty years. It is partly in the spirit of wanting to share something of what I learned at Borges's side that I now bring these pieces together.

Appendix:
A Footnote to Infamy
A Chronology and Guide to Borges's
Universal History of Infamy

Jorge Luis Borges became world-famous, ultimately, as a writer of short stories. More remarkable is the fact that his production was so small. The reputation is based on the thirty-four stories written between 1933 and 1953. His first collection, *El jardín de los senderos que se bifurcan* (The Garden of Branching Paths), issued early in 1942, must stand as the most revolutionary set of short fiction since Joyce's *Dubliners*, published twenty-eight years earlier. Borges, as I hope these pages will show, came to the short story in an inconspicuous, tentative, roundabout fashion, groping his way with sketches and borrowings. In fact, he sneaked in by the back door via an amalgam of the essay, the book review, and the hoax. Among the great writers of our time, it is difficult to recall a more timorous debut.

I: CHRONOLOGY

1933 – (12 August) The Buenos Aires daily *Crítica* launches a Saturday supplement offering popular entertainment in the form of light fiction, humour, puzzles, and, from time to time, comic strips. The material is generously, even gaudily, printed in colour. The thirty-four-year-old Borges is among the editors of this sheet. To its maiden issue he contributes the first of a series of fictionalized biographies of villains and scoundrels. This opener, on an American slave-stealer of the 1830s, is entitled 'HISTORIA UNIVERSAL DE LA INFAMIA [:] El Espantoso Redentor Lazarus Morell'.

(19 August) *Crítica* prints Borges's second instalment of villainy. The subject this time is a turn-of-the-century Jewish-American gangster, Edward Eastman né Osterman. The piece is called 'HISTORIA UNIVERSAL DE LA INFAMIA [:] Eastman, el Proveedor de Iniquidades'.

(26 August) In less screaming typography, *Crítica* presents instalment three, 'Historia Universal de la Infamia [:] La Viuda Ching'. She is a lady buccaneer who ranges the China coast in the first decade of the last century. When she makes her debut in book form two years later, Borges dubs her 'La viuda Ching, Pirata Punctual'.

(2 September) For five issues the series waits. Meanwhile, *Crítica* publishes a piece called 'El Brujo Postergado', which many readers surely recognize

as a version of an old classic of Spain, slightly condensed and translated into modern Spanish. The contribution is unsigned.

(16 September) *Crítica* publishes a short story by an unknown writer named F. Bustos. Its title is 'Hombres de las orillas' (Men from the Edge of Town), and it is destined to become one of the most famous works of contemporary Argentine fiction. When it is reprinted in book form two years later (as 'Hombre de la esquina rosada'), F. Bustos turns out to have been Jorge Luis Borges. Of this episode, Borges wrote in his autobiography:

It took me six years, from 1927 to 1933, to go from that all too self-conscious sketch 'Hombres pelearon' to my first outright short story, 'Hombre de la esquina rosada' (Streetcorner Man). A friend of mine, don Nicolás Paredes, a former political boss and professional gambler of the Northside, had died, and I wanted to record something of his voice, his anecdotes, and his particular way of telling them. I slaved over my every page, sounding out each sentence and striving to phrase it in his exact tones. We were living out in Adrogué at the time and, because I knew my mother would heartily disapprove of the subject matter, I composed in secret over a period of several months.... But out of shyness, and perhaps a feeling that the story was a bit beneath me, I signed it with a pen-name – the name of one of my great-great grandfathers, Francisco Bustos.

(30 September) *Crítica* resumes its infamy series with the appearance of 'Historia Universal de la Infamia [:] El Impostor Inverosímil Tom Castro'. Our shady hero on this occasion is the Tichborne Claimant; the setting, Valparaiso, Sydney, Paris, and London. In the same number appears a short tale, which purports to be quoted from Captain Richard F. Burton, the English translator of the Arabian Nights. It is called 'El espejo de tinta' and is, of course, unsigned.

(2 December) 'La Cámera de las Estatuas [:] (Traducido de un texto árabe del siglo XIII)' appears in *Crítica*. We are not told who translated this thirteenth-century Arabic tale.

(9 December) The *Crítica* series makes its last appearance as such, portraying an eighteenth-century scoundrel from the imperial court of Japan. The title (in blaring caps once more): 'HISTORIA UNIVERSAL DE LA INFAMIA [:] El Incivil Maestro de Ceremonias Kôtsuké no Suké'.

1934 – (20 January) *Crítica* publishes a story by Borges called 'El Rostro del Profeta'. While it has all the earmarks of the infamy series (it is about the Veiled Prophet of Khurasan), can any signficance be attached to the fact that it does not bear the series' title?

(23 June) Two brief unsigned tales are published in the *Crítica* supplement – 'El Teólogo' (retitled 'Un teólogo en la muerte' for its appearance in book form the next year) and '2 Que Soñaron' (later retitled 'Historia de los dos que soñaron').

1935 – (July or August) Editorial Tor brings out as the third volume in its Coleccion Megáfono *Historia universal de la infamia*. In addition to the twelve forementioned pieces, it prints the story of another infamous character – the well-known desperado from the American Southwest, Billy the Kid – under the title 'El asesino desinteresado Bill Harrigan'. Harrigan? But everyone knows that Billy the Kid was William H. Bonney. The book, however, sheds light on several points and tidies up a mystery or two. An appended bibliography lists nine volumes and an encyclopedia as the sources of the seven pieces that form the title section, 'A Universal History of Infamy'. The encyclopedia and eight of the books are in English; the ninth, in German. The mysteries dispelled: *A Universal History*'s second section, 'Hombre de la esquina rosada', omits any mention of the unknown F. Bustos; and a third section, called 'Etcetera', while collecting the five unsigned tales from *Crítica*, reveals their origins – two are from the Thousand and One Nights; one from a rare Burton volume of African exploration, *The Lake Regions of Equatorial Africa*; one from an encyclopedic work by

Swedenborg; and one from the Infante Don Juan Manuel. Or so we are told. In a preface confirming these attributions, Borges claims that he has 'no other rights to them than those of translator and reader.' Of this first and only printing of the Editorial Tor edition, two hundred and fifty copies are issued. *A Universal History of Infamy* is Borges's tenth published book and his first of narrative prose.

1946 – (January) A new sixty-four-page monthly called *Los Anales de Buenos Aires* publishes its first number. Unlike *Crítica*, it is well printed on good paper, and it has no popular pretensions. Borges, now forty-six, is its editor, although his name does not appear as such until the third issue.

(March) *Los Anales de Buenos Aires* publishes a four-page collection of literary oddities under the heading MUSEO. Among the ten snippets is one called 'Del rigor en la ciencia', attributed to a certain 'Suárez Miranda' as an excerpt from *Viajes de Varones Prudentes* (Travels of Praiseworthy Men).

(May) The second instalment of MUSEO pieces appears in *Los Anales de Buenos Aires*. This time their collector is listed as 'B. Lynch Davis'. Among the pieces is 'Un doble de Mahoma'. 'B. Lynch Davis' is a pseudonym for Borges and Adolfo Bioy Casares. 'Lynch' and 'Davis' are both ancestral names of Bioy's.

(October) 'B. Lynch Davis' collects in his MUSEO a poem called 'El enemigo generoso'. It is ascribed to H. Gering's *Anhang zur Heimskringla*.

1954 – (November or December) The Buenos Aires publisher Emecé publishes a new and enlarged edition of *Historia universal de la infamia* as the third volume in its series of Borges's works. This second edition of the book includes a new preface as well as the three pieces from *Los Anales*. *Historia universal* is reprinted at least eight times in the next eighteen years, and it also appears in a cheaper pocket edition. Of this 1954 reissue, Borges writes that 'The book is no more than appearance, than a surface of images; for that reason, it may prove enjoyable.'

II: GUIDE

Translators, reviewers, and students of Borges have long been puzzled or mistaken about what in the infamy stories belongs to Borges and what does not. The author himself, as was not uncharacteristic of him, contributed to the general bewilderment by variously belittling or disclaiming the book. In its opening pages he even went so far as to lay false tracks in the path of the independent investigator. Thoroughly understood, *A Universal History of Infamy* sheds valuable light on the origins of Borges's subsequent, much-admired fiction. To this end, the notes that follow – gleanings of a special relationship to both author and book – set out to reveal hidden or not easily accessible sources and to point out hitherto unconfirmed (and possibly undetected) hoaxes.

Where the sources are brief, and where they and Borges mainly coincide (as in the cases of Tom Castro and the Tichborne Claimant, and Kôtsuké no Suké and A.B. Mitford's 'The Forty-seven Rónins'), I offer no comment.

'A Universal History of Infamy'

'The Dread Redeemer Lazarus Morell' – The prime source is Chapter Twenty-nine of Mark Twain's *Life on the Mississippi*. The excerpt from Morell's writing (pp. 28–9 of the Penguin edition)* is found there. Numerous incidental details are lifted from various other chapters. The amount of mud disgorged by the river (p. 20), for example, is from the opening of Twain; the description of the 'great raft as big as the sky, with a cabin at the point or three or four wigwams' (p. 25), from Chapter Three. Among the marks of pure Borges are the elaborate depiction of Morell, whose published daguerreotypes, we are told, are 'not authentic' (p. 22); and the catalogue of the runaway slave's ultimate deliverance (pp. 26–7).

---

* Unless otherwise noted, all pages subsequently cited refer to this edition.

Little, if anything, appears to have been used from De Voto's *Mark Twain's America*, which serves only to air Borges's reading and to pad the bibliography.

'The Widow Ching, Lady Pirate' – The opening sentence of the Spanish text is a topical allusion to a Spanish *zarzuela*, *Las corsarias*, which had toured Buenos Aires two or three years before the Borges piece was written. Mary Read, Anne Bonney, and John Rackham (pp. 41–2) are to be found in Philip Gosse's *History of Piracy*, which is also the source for the widow herself. Various bits of Gosse, whether or not pertaining to the widow, were plundered from an entire chapter on Japanese and Chinese pirates. The widow's code (pp. 44–5) is freely adapted from Gosse, but the imperial decree (p. 46) is all Borges. The phrasing, 'Its style was widely criticized' (p. 45) – a Borges signature – tips us off to this. The closing quote is also from Gosse.

'Monk Eastman, Purveyer of Iniquities' – The long catalogue of the old New York underworld's pictureque inhabitants (pp. 51–3) is from Herbert Asbury's *Gangs of New York*: the bits are culled from a dozen and a half different places, beginning on page thirteen and running all the way to page three hundred and fifty-nine. Monk himself, of course, is featured in Asbury. The short catalogue describing the hundred embattled gunmen (pp. 56–7) is an injection of Borges's own ironic humour. What these men felt on entering the shoot-out ('that if the

first shots did not hit them they were invulnerable'
(p. 57) derives from information given to Borges by
Nicolás Paredes, the former political boss, whom the
author knew from the Palermo neighbourhood of
Buenos Aires. The notion is repeated many years later
in *Doctor Brodie's Report* (p. 40, Penguin edition):
'The man who is not wounded at the outset thinks
himself invulnerable.'

'The Disinterested Killer Bill Harrigan' – Bill Bonney, history's Billy the Kid, was born in New York
City, but nothing is known of his life there, for at the
age of three his family emigrated to Kansas. We find
in Asbury another Billy the Kid, a New York hoodlum. Borges has grafted Walter Burns's *Saga of Billy
the Kid*. The exchange with Garrett about 'Shooting
tin cans and men' (p. 66) is from Burns, as are several
background details. Not, however, Billy's death and
wake. The piece is about equal parts Asbury, Burns,
and Borges. Frederick Watson's *Century of Gunmen*
contributes an entry to the list of sources and no
more.

'The Masked Dyer, Hakim of Merv', entirely of
Borges's own creation, exposes the deception of the
1954 preface. There Borges claims his book to be
the irresponsible game of a young man who falsi-
fied and distorted 'the tales of others.' The fact of
the piece's total originality may explain why it did
not bear the 'Universal History' heading when it
appeared in *Crítica*, although typographical consid-

erations or sheer carelessness were more likely the real reason. The few lines about the Veiled Prophet in Sir Percy Sykes's *History of Persia* provide nothing. Thomas Moore's poem, mentioned by both Sykes and Borges, seems to have provided two minor details. (See Moore, lines 25 and footnote, and 179–82.) The *Vernichtung der Rose*, the German work listed as one of the sources and long a puzzle to everyone, is a hoax. Alexander Schulz, its supposed author, stands for Borges's friend Xul Solar, whose real name was Alejandro Schulz Solari. Once these things are known, Borges's sole authorship is obvious. The erudition of the first page, complete with the revelation of a forgery; the matter quoted from the Arabic codex (pp. 78–9) and the prophet's holy book (p. 84); the invention of a cosmogony 'in which borrowings from old Gnostic beliefs are nonetheless detectable' (p. 83) – all these are Borges's sleight-of-hand. There is another Borges hallmark here: in making fun of Hakim's plagiarism, Borges pokes fun at himself, for it was he who borrowed from the Gnostics to create the tenets of the Veiled Prophet's creed. See in Borges's 1931 essay 'Una vindicación del falso Basilides', published in *Discusión*, the overlapping elements in the cosmogonies of the Gnostic heresiarch and the Khurusan impostor. In the Hakim piece, also, is the line about mirrors and abominations (p. 83), made famous on its second appearance, a few years later, in 'Tlön,

Uqbar, Orbis Tertius'. 'Hakim of Merv' is the first
Borges Borges.

'Streetcorner Man'

Cutting out the dead man's intestines to keep him
from floating (p. 100) has its origin in Lazarus
Morell's account of his journey to Natchez (p. 29).
This lurid detail is also cited in De Voto. Borges has
himself written about the background, sources, and
composition of 'Streetcorner Man' in *The Aleph and
Other Stories 1933–1969* (pp. 150–1 and 170–1,
Picador edition).

'Etcetera'

'A Theologian in Death' – This is Swedenborg
though not, as Borges has credited it, from the multi-
volumed *Arcana Coelestia*. The actual source is section
797 of *True Christian Religion* (*Vera Christiana Religio*).
Why the dissimulation? To lay a false track, not to
mention the irresistibleness of a title like *Arcana
Coelestia*.

'The Chamber of Statues' is Burton's 'The City of
Labtayt', from his version of the Thousand and One
Nights (IV, 99–101), and it forms parts of nights 271
and 272. Borges has filled out the original perfunctory tale and given it dramatic form. Note the prototype Aleph in the fifth chamber: 'a circular mirror

… whose worth was priceless … and he who looked into it could see the face of his fathers and his sons from the first Adam down to those who shall hear the Trumpet' (p. 109). In Burton, this reads: 'a marvelous mirror … wherein who so looked might see the counterfeit presentiment of the seven climates of the world….' Burton's mirror is mentioned on the last page of Borges's celebrated story 'The Aleph', written in 1945: 'the mirror that Tariq ibn-Ziyad found in a tower (*Thousand and One Nights*, 272)….' Borges's 'vizier' and 'emirs' (p. 107) are 'grandees' in Burton. Burton's term is the correct one, for they were Spanish noblemen and not Muslim officials who would have warned their king against what might befall them at the hands of Arabs. To correct this discrepancy and yet retain the colourful words 'vizier' and 'emir', Borges and I wrote the tale's short opening paragraph especially for the English translation. It is this use of Muslim terms that constitutes the 'internal evidence' mentioned there.

'The Tale of the Two Dreamers' – The source is the complete Burton, vol. IV, p. 289 (reprinted in the Modern Library's *Arabian Nights*, pp. 333–4). Compare the opening of Borges's second paragraph (p. 111) with the opening of his story 'The Two Kings and Their Two Labyrinths', in *The Aleph and Other Stories*, which Borges has characterized as 'a page – overlooked by Lane or Burton – out of the *Arabian Nights*.'

'The Wizard Postponed' – This magnificent piece is the heart of Don Juan Manuel's 'Enxiemplo XI' in his *Libro de los enxiemplos del Conde Lucanor et de Patronio* (1335). Borges has noted that a similar tale figures in the Arabian collection *The Forty Days and Forty Nights*.

'The Mirror of Ink' has nothing whatever to do with Burton. It is pure, original Borges and gives the lie to the statement in the Preface to the First Edition that 'As for the examples of magic that close the volume, I have no other rights to them than those of translator and reader.' The opening paragraph of the tale, in which an elaborate source is presented for the story about to be told, prefigures later Borges. The mirror of ink, the device itself, comes from Edward William Lane's *Manners and Customs of the Modern Egyptians* (Everyman's Library edition, pp. 274–82), one of Borges's favourite books. What is seen in the pool of ink, however, is of Borges's own invention, not Lane's. We have here another Aleph – this time, a full-fledged prototype. Compare the items seen in the mirror of ink (p. 123) with those of the catalogue in the 1945 Aleph (*Aleph and Other Stories*, pp. 20–1). The 'whale that dies on hearing the cry of a man' comes from a poem by the Argentine Leopoldo Lugones. Borges cites some rare Burton volumes – which he never laid eyes on – as the source of this story. Their title is *The Lake Regions of Central Africa* and not, as Borges had it, with the word 'Equatorial' instead of 'Central'. I corrected this in the American edition of the translation, but later, in a biography of Burton, I found both adjectives given in the title. I copied the mistake, alas, in the Allen Lane edition of *A Universal History*.

'A Double for Mohammed' is from Swedenborg's *True Christian Religion*, sections 829 and 830. The Borges version is very nearly a straightforward translation.

'The Generous Enemy' – The poem is by Borges and reflects his long interest in the old language and literature of Norway and Iceland. 'Barfod' means 'barefoot', or 'bareleg', from the king's having brought to Norway the Scottish and Irish custom of wearing the kilt. Magnus ruled as king of Norway from 1094 to 1103. H. Gering and his supplement to the *Heimskringla* are fictitious.

'Of Exactitude in Science' – Again the listed source is a fiction. This famous paragraph was written by Borges together with Adolfo Bioy Casares, which I acknowledge in the translation (p. 131) by endowing Suárez Miranda with the initials J(orge) A(dolfo). The idea for the piece was inspired by Josiah Royce's *The World and the Individual* (1899).

Borges wrote that his infamy pieces were never meant for book publication but only for 'popular consumption' in the pages of *Crítica*. I am not sure I believe him. His copy of *The Gangs of New York*, which he gave me, bears his signature and the date August 1932 – exactly one year before *Crítica* began to publish its Saturday supplement and his piece on Lazarus Morell first appeared. Borges made me a gift of another of his books, *Carrying a Gun for Al Capone* (subtitled 'The intimate Experiences of a Gangster in the bodyguard of Al Capone'), Jack Bilbo's account of his life as an associate of Al Capone's. The copy bears Borges's minuscule signature and the date 1933. He told me that he once planned a sketch on Capone for his infamy series. Though he never wrote it, mentions of Capone occur in two different sketches in *A Universal History* (pp. 24 and 55). The first of the references even has about it a promise of more to follow.

Another of the books of this period that Borges presented me with, William Bolitho's *Murder for Profit*, is signed and dated 1935. The volume profiles five once-famous European professional murderers. It is possible that Borges acquired it as source material for further infamy sketches. Whether he did or not, my copy yields up a useful nugget. It was Borges's habit to use the free and paste-down back endpapers of his books on which to make notes. (After the onset of his blindness these were in his mother's hand.) They made up a kind of personal index and sometimes, in the case of poems, consisted of no more than brief quotes. At the back of the Bolitho volume, Borges wrote, '*efecto, quizá demasiado evidente, obtenido por puntuación – 34.*' Meaning, or referring to, an effect too readily derived from a use of punctuation. On p. 34 of the text, in the course of two sentences, the author makes a series of six statements, each followed by a bracketed counterpoint. For instance: '... from his bed (because he is alone) Burke takes the pillow (because it is at hand)', etc. While appearing to express disapproval of the practice here, Borges was not averse to adopting, toning down, and making great use – and sometimes overuse – of it himself, as can be seen in *A Universal History* and throughout his next collection of narrative prose, *The Garden of Branching Paths*.

The evidence is that Borges had been reading up and been planning pieces on infamous characters for some time before and maybe after the *Crítica* sketches were run. He conveniently forgot all this, I suspect, as a cover for his shame over a volume he could no longer justify. Some of his harsh judgement of the book is valid. *A Universal History of Infamy* was an exercise, a proving ground, and no doubt after the achievement of his following set of stories it must have appeared to him too humble an effort, too feeble a start. But I think in the end we must contradict him and recognize that these sketches helped release Borges to fulfil his destiny.

NORMAN THOMAS DI GIOVANNI met Borges at Harvard, in 1967, when they began working together on English versions of the Argentine writer's poems. Upon Borges's invitation, di Giovanni moved to Buenos Aires a year later. Their collaborative efforts appeared for nine years in the *New Yorker* magazine and were celebrated throughout the English-speaking world.

A critic wrote, 'What can one say in regard to the collaboration between Borges and di Giovanni …? It is so evidently effective, so tacitly perfect. They are not translating; they are writing together and, what's more, they are having fun. So does the reader. May the two of them go on forever.' And a noted academic offered this praise: '… Norman Thomas di Giovanni has rendered a most felicitous service to Borges. His dedication, his quality as a writer, and the fact that Borges has been willing to collaborate with him, all these factors have produced results of which the author, the translator and the publisher can be proud.'

And yet when Borges died, in 1986, his Estate commissioned new translations and has refused to grant permission for the collaboration with Borges to be reprinted. Their work, in effect, has been airbrushed out of history.

Down the years, di Giovanni has been rewarded by a number of foundation grants, among them a Guggenheim Fellowship. *The Lesson of the Master*, his memoir of Borges and essays on his work, offers a unique insight into one of the most unusual and acclaimed literary partnerships of the twentieth century.

For this, the Argentine government in 1991 appointed di Giovanni a Commander of the Order of May, their highest cultural honour.

Also in the Library of Lost Books is di Giovanni's edition and translation, with Susan Ashe, of *The Slaughteryard*, the Argentine classic by Esteban Echeverría.

from which your national literature flows, Peron, Peronism, the juntas, and the strongmen who litter the history of the Argentine seem utterly predictable. All the stuff in the appendixes is brilliant too. This is an excellent book and deserves to be read widely.

– Carlo Gébler

The translation is excellent, as I expected, but particularly useful are the glossary and the appendixes. *The Slaughteryard* is one of the most famous short stories in Spanish American literature, yet for decades people read around its most shocking detail, namely the intention of anal rape of a man by other men. The *mazorca* references are unequivocal. Other references to *palo* and *verga* suggest even greater sexual content. You have done us a great service by putting all this material in one book.

– Nicolas Shumway

The Slaughteryard is a powerful and memorable tale, packed with information and colour, observation and, above all, political indictment. Translated with enormous vigour by erstwhile Borges collaborator and translator Norman Thomas di Giovanni and Susan Ashe, it provides an insight into a world that's both recognisably modern and tantalisingly 'other', which is just what you expect from a classic 'lost book'. If you stop at the story, you'll already have had value for money. If you decide to read the rest of the book as well, you'll come away not only wiser but also irresistibly entertained. It's packed with gems. The book not only introduces and contextualises one of South America's greatest stories but also delights on its own terms. I recommend it.

– Charles Lambert

Fortunately . . . di Giovanni has supplied a substantial introduction and glossary which do an excellent job of providing context (and there's a lot of context to provide). The result is a powerful piece of work. The presentation of *The Slaughteryard* in this volume is an excellent example of how to make an old text accessible to contemporary general readers whilst still allowing them to discover that text for themselves.

– David Hebblethwaite

The Borges Legacy
by Kaiser Haq

Norman Thomas di Giovanni's collaborative translations of Jorge Luis Borges belong in the realm of legend rather than mundane literary history. The story begins in Harvard, 1967-68. Borges, already world famous and partially available in English translations, albeit of uneven merit, is in residence as Charles Eliot Norton Professor of Poetry. Di Giovanni has just won his spurs as a translator and editor with a selection from the Spanish poet Jorge Guillén. Bowled over by Borges' *Obra Poética* (Poetical Works), he writes to the poet, proposing to edit a selection translated by di Giovanni himself and others; among them would be John Hollander, Richard Howard, W.S. Merwin, Alastair Reid, John Updike and Richard Wilbur. Uncharacteristically, Borges writes back; the project gets going at once.

Unlike previous translators, di Giovanni makes full use of Borges' mastery of English; the two put their heads together to produce English versions that read like originals. Di Giovanni moves to Buenos Aires and the collaborative effort goes on for nearly five years, resulting in the translation of eleven books, most prose fiction. In the process di Giovanni nudges Borges into a fresh burst of creativity. One interesting product is a 65-page collaborative autobiography, written directly in English. Di Giovanni tells the story of his literary adventures with Borges in *The Lesson of the Master*, an engaging mix of memoir, scholarship and criticism, indispensable to the Borges buff; it is also an excellent lesson in the art of writing.

The story has an unpleasant surprise ending, though. Weeks before his death, the terminally ill Borges marries María Kodama, 38 years his junior and leaves her his estate. She loses no time in renegotiating translation rights to the entire Borges oeuvre, at the same time cancelling the rights for the collaborative work done with di Giovanni. The reason obviously is pecuniary; but for Kodama's gain it's the student of literature who has to pay a price. It's a supreme irony that the Borges estate has withddrawn from print a rich trove of Borges texts that are canonical by any definition of the term.

Di Giovanni, however, continues to mine his Borges legacy,

a spiritual, literary legacy as his splendid new translated volume testifies. It was Borges who drew his attention to certain nineteenth-century Argentine writers and for good measure presented him with editions of their works. One of the five acknowledged masterpieces from that period is Esteban Echeverría's story 'El Matadero' ('The Slaughteryard'). It is only 30 pages long, just long enough for a pamphlet. Di Giovanni presents it as the pièce de résistance in a literary and cultural feast, and follows it up with a wholesome salad of notes in a Glossary. The Spanish original is included as a side dish, a bonus for students of the language.

For starters di Giovanni succinctly places Echeverría's career in its historical context. Argentina attained independence from Spain in 1816, only to explode into civil war. Two powerful factions evolved. On one side the Unitarians (not to be confused with the Christian denomination of that name), with their bastion in cosmopolitan Buenos Aires, were squarely in the tradition of European liberalism, and favoured a strong central government; on the other hand the Federalists, many of them ranch owning caudillos, were conservative (to put it mildly) and wanted local autonomy. The Federalist caudillo Juan Manuel de Rosas emerged as the strongman, and save for a three-year interregnum, ruled with an iron hand from 1829 to 1852. Echeverría, like Borges' ancestors, was a staunch Unitarian, and fled into exile in Uruguay, leaving behind his manuscripts; not long after, at 45, he was dead.

'El Matadero' was first published in a journal in 1871, to wide acclaim; and is now said to be the most widely used school text in Hispanic America. The story is set towards the end of the 1830s during Lent. The Church's interdiction on meat eating, in a land addicted to beef, produces dangerous withdrawal symptoms. Lest the discontent take a political turn, Church and government ease up and allow the slaughter of fifty head of cattle at the Alto slaughteryard. It has been raining heavily for days, evoking apocalyptic thoughts. The account explicitly alludes to the Deluge; and to at least one reader, it looks forward to another famous deluge in Latin American fiction: in García Márquez's *One Hundred Years of Solitude*.

The Alto is an infernal quagmire whose denizens are monstrous characters, rabid Federalists all. The symbolism is clear and it gains in power through the vivid description. The horrible slaughter is nearly over when a mounted stranger comes cantering down. The knife-wielding slaughteryard louts identify him from his clothes and appearance as a Unitarian: colours worn and styles of keeping facial hair were signifiers in Argentine political semiotics. They take him by surprise, so that his pistol is of no avail. He is strapped down, subjected to a burlesque trial, and martyred through murderous play. Till the end he heroically affirms the liberal Unitarian creed and roundly condemns the Federalist barbarians. Admittedly, 'The Slaughteryard' has a naive, propagandist aspect, but this is more than offset by the relentless naturalism of the descriptions and a dash of mordant satire.

Seven appendices make up a divers dessert tray: there is Juan Gutiérrez's foreword to the first edition of the story; accounts of contemporary travellers, Darwin among them; bloodthirsty Federalist verses; and poems about the Federalist tyranny by Echeverría and his fellow Unitarian Ascasubi. They significantly enhance our understanding and appreciation of the story.

The Envoi offers the meditative brandy and cigar to round off the feast. Di Giovanni highlights the continuing relevance of 'The Slaughteryard' to contemporary Argentina and, indeed, to the whole world, a point those of us who lived through the Bangladesh independence war of 1971 will well appreciate; he himself saw at first hand a latter-day manifestation of the kind of tyranny depicted in the story in recent Argentine military dictatorships, and notes with chagrin that even Borges publicly hailed the dictator General Videla. The moving final paragraph will strike a chord in every – if I may borrow a phrase from Adrian Mitchell – 'heart on the left':

'Reading and re-reading Echeverría gives us a sense of innocent individuals in their thousands crowding round with unvoiced voices – Argentines of Rosas' time and since – desperate for recognition and redress, desperate to be heard. To all such victims we have a debt of honour, just as we have a debt of honour everywhere and in every age to victims of social injustice.'

The Star Magazine (Dhaka)